Table of Content

Chapter 1: Introduction to Rabbit Genetics

11 What is Genetics?

Genetics is the scientific study of heredity and variation in living organisms. It seeks to understand the mechanisms of inheritance, the genetic basis of traits and diseases, and the genetic diversity within and between populations. By delving into the molecular and cellular processes that govern the transmission of genetic information, genetics provides crucial insights into the development, function, and evolution of living systems.

At its core, genetics revolves around the concept of genes. Genes are discrete units of DNA, the molecule that carries genetic information. Each gene contains the instructions for constructing a specific protein or molecule, which play essential roles in determining the traits and characteristics of an organism. Genes are passed down from parents to offspring through reproduction, providing the blueprint for each individual's unique genetic makeup.

The field of genetics encompasses a wide range of disciplines, from molecular biology to population genetics and evolutionary biology. Molecular genetics focuses on the structure, function, and regulation of genes at the molecular level, examining the interplay between DNA, RNA, and proteins. Through techniques such as gene sequencing and gene editing, molecular geneticists unravel the genetic basis of traits and diseases, paving the way for personalized medicine and genetic therapies.

Population genetics, on the other hand, studies the genetic variation within populations and its implications for evolution. By examining the distribution of alleles, the alternative forms of genes, within a population, population geneticists can infer patterns of inheritance, genetic diversity, and the forces that shape them. This knowledge is crucial for understanding the dynamics of populations, predicting their response to environmental changes, and conserving genetic resources.

Evolutionary genetics takes a broader perspective, investigating the role of genetic variation in the evolution of species. By studying the changes in allele frequencies over generations and the impact of these changes on fitness, evolutionary geneticists unravel the genetic mechanisms that drive adaptation, speciation, and the diversification of life on Earth. Their research provides insights into the origins of new species, the history of life, and the processes that shape the intricate tapestry of biodiversity.

In addition to these core disciplines, genetics also extends into other areas of biology and medicine. Medical genetics investigates the genetic basis of human diseases and disorders, seeking to identify genetic risk factors, develop diagnostic tools, and devise treatments. Forensic genetics uses genetic information for identification purposes in criminal investigations and paternity testing. Agricultural genetics applies genetic principles to improve crop yields, enhance livestock production, and develop new varieties of plants and animals.

Genetics has revolutionized our understanding of living organisms, providing a deeper appreciation of the mechanisms that govern heredity, evolution, and disease. Its advancements have led to groundbreaking applications in medicine, agriculture, and biotechnology, improving human health, enhancing food security, and paving the way for new technologies. As our knowledge of genetics continues to grow, we can expect even more transformative discoveries that will shape the future of biology and medicine.

12 Why Study Rabbit Genetics?

The study of rabbit genetics offers a multifaceted and rewarding endeavor for both researchers and enthusiasts alike. Its significance lies in the numerous benefits it provides, ranging from enhancing our understanding of fundamental biological principles to driving practical applications in various fields.

Unraveling the Mysteries of Inheritance:

Rabbit genetics serves as a powerful tool for investigating the intricate mechanisms of inheritance. By studying the transmission of traits from parents to offspring, researchers can elucidate the underlying genetic principles governing the expression of inherited characteristics. This knowledge has far-reaching implications for our comprehension of genetic disorders, disease susceptibility, and evolutionary processes.

Advancing Medical Research:

The rabbit has emerged as an important model organism in biomedical research. Its genetic similarity to humans makes it an invaluable resource for studying human diseases and developing novel therapeutic strategies. By manipulating rabbit genes and observing the resulting phenotypes, scientists can gain insights into the genetic basis of complex disorders such as cardiovascular disease, obesity, and cancer.

Improving Animal Welfare and Production:

The application of genetic principles in rabbit production has led to significant advancements in animal welfare and productivity. Through selective breeding programs, breeders can improve desirable traits such as growth rate, meat quality, litter size, and disease resistance. By understanding the genetic mechanisms underlying these traits, researchers can develop more efficient and sustainable breeding practices.

Preserving Biodiversity:

Genetic diversity is essential for the survival and adaptability of species. Rabbit genetics plays a crucial role in identifying and preserving genetic diversity within rabbit populations. This knowledge is vital for conservation efforts aimed at protecting endangered species and maintaining healthy ecosystems.

Educational Value:

The study of rabbit genetics offers a valuable educational tool for students and individuals of all ages. It provides a tangible way to explore concepts in genetics, inheritance, and evolution. Through hands-on activities and experiments, students can witness the power of genetic principles and gain a deeper appreciation for the intricacies of life.

Practical Applications in Other Fields:

The principles and techniques developed through rabbit genetics research have found widespread application in other fields, including forensic science, biotechnology, and agriculture. For example, genetic analysis of rabbit DNA has proven useful in identifying individuals in criminal investigations, understanding the genetic basis of crop improvement, and developing genetically modified organisms. It contributes to our understanding of fundamental biological principles, drives advancements in medical research, improves animal welfare and production, preserves biodiversity, provides educational value, and finds applications in various other fields. As the field continues to evolve, it holds the promise of even greater insights and breakthroughs in the years to come.

13 Basic Genetic Concepts: Genes, Alleles, Genotype, Phenotype

Genetics is the study of genes, which are the units of heredity in living organisms. Genes are responsible for passing on traits from parents to offspring. Each gene is located at a specific locus, or position, on a chromosome. Chromosomes are thread-like structures that are found in the nucleus of cells.

Genes

Genes are made up of DNA, which is a molecule that

contains the instructions for making proteins. Proteins are the building blocks of cells and are responsible for a wide range of functions, such as metabolism, growth, and reproduction.

Each gene codes for a specific protein. The instructions for making a protein are divided into units called codons. Each codon consists of three nucleotides, which are the building blocks of DNA. The sequence of codons in a gene determines the sequence of amino acids in the protein that is produced.

Alleles

Alleles are different forms of a gene. For example, one allele of the gene for eye color may code for brown eyes, while another allele may code for blue eyes. Each cell contains two copies of each gene, one copy inherited from each parent.

If the two alleles of a gene are the same, the individual is said to be homozygous for that gene. If the two alleles of a gene are different, the individual is said to be heterozygous for that gene.

Genotype

The genotype of an individual is the combination of alleles that they have for a particular gene. For example, an individual who is homozygous for the brown eye allele would have a genotype of BB. An individual who is heterozygous for the brown eye and blue eye alleles would have a genotype of Bb.

Phenotype

The phenotype of an individual is the observable

characteristics of the individual. The phenotype is determined by the genotype of the individual, as well as by environmental factors.

For example, the phenotype of an individual with the genotype BB would be brown eyes. The phenotype of an individual with the genotype Bb would be either brown eyes or blue eyes, depending on which allele is dominant.

Dominant and Recessive Alleles

In some cases, one allele of a gene is dominant over the other allele. This means that the dominant allele will be expressed in the phenotype of the individual, even if the individual is heterozygous for the gene. The recessive allele will only be expressed in the phenotype of the individual if the individual is homozygous for the recessive allele.

For example, the brown eye allele is dominant over the blue eye allele. This means that an individual with the genotype Bb will have brown eyes, even though they have one copy of the blue eye allele. An individual with the genotype bb will have blue eyes.

Codominance

In some cases, neither allele of a gene is dominant over the other allele. This is called codominance. In cases of codominance, both alleles are expressed in the phenotype of the individual.

For example, the allele for the A blood type is codominant with the allele for the B blood type. This means that an individual with the genotype AB will have both A and B antigens on their red blood cells.

Incomplete Dominance

In some cases, one allele of a gene is not completely
dominant over the other allele. This is called incomplete
dominance. In cases of incomplete dominance, the
phenotype of the individual is a blend of the phenotypes of
the two homozygous individuals.

For example, the allele for red flowers is incompletely
dominant over the allele for white flowers. This means that
an individual with the genotype Rr will have pink flowers.

14 Mendelian Inheritance: The Foundation of Rabbit Genetics

Gregor Mendel, an Austrian monk, is considered the father
of modern genetics. His work with pea plants in the mid-
19th century laid the foundation for our understanding of
inheritance. Mendel's principles of inheritance, known as
Mendelian inheritance, have been shown to apply to all
living organisms, including rabbits.

1. 4. 1 Mendel's Laws of Inheritance

Mendel's laws of inheritance are based on his experiments
with pea plants. He observed that each trait is controlled by
two factors, which we now call genes. Each gene can have
different versions, called alleles. For example, the gene for
flower color in pea plants can have two alleles: one for red
flowers and one for white flowers.

Mendel's first law, the law of segregation, states that the two
alleles for a gene segregate (separate) during the formation

of gametes (eggs and sperm). This means that each gamete will carry only one allele for each gene.

Mendel's second law, the law of independent assortment, states that the alleles for different genes assort independently of each other during the formation of gametes. This means that the inheritance of one gene does not influence the inheritance of another gene.

1. 4. 2 Mendelian Inheritance in Rabbits

Mendelian inheritance has been well-studied in rabbits. Many different traits in rabbits, such as coat color, fur texture, and ear shape, are controlled by single genes.

For example, the gene for coat color in rabbits has two alleles: one for black coat color and one for white coat color. A rabbit that inherits two copies of the black allele will have a black coat. A rabbit that inherits two copies of the white allele will have a white coat. A rabbit that inherits one copy of each allele will have a coat that is a mixture of black and white, known as agouti.

The inheritance of coat color in rabbits is a simple example of Mendelian inheritance. However, many other traits in rabbits are controlled by more complex genetic mechanisms.

1. 4. 3 Applications of Mendelian Inheritance in Rabbit Breeding

Mendelian inheritance is a valuable tool for rabbit breeders. By understanding the genetic basis of different traits, breeders can select for desired traits and avoid undesirable traits.

For example, a breeder who wants to produce rabbits with a specific coat color can use Mendelian inheritance to predict the probability of obtaining that color in their offspring. A breeder who wants to avoid producing rabbits with a certain genetic defect can use Mendelian inheritance to select against that defect.

Mendelian inheritance is also used in rabbit genetics research. By studying the inheritance of different traits, researchers can learn more about the genetic basis of those traits and how they are controlled.

1. 4. 4 Conclusion

Mendelian inheritance is the foundation of rabbit genetics. By understanding the principles of Mendelian inheritance, breeders and researchers can better understand the genetic basis of different traits and how they are inherited. This knowledge can be used to improve rabbit breeding practices and to advance our understanding of rabbit genetics.

Chapter 2: Understanding Rabbit Breeds and their Traits

21 The Importance of Breed Standards

In the realm of purebred dog breeding, the concept of breed standards holds paramount importance. These meticulously crafted guidelines serve as the blueprint for each recognized breed, outlining the physical, temperamental, and behavioral characteristics that define its identity. Adherence to breed standards ensures the preservation of the unique heritage and purpose of each breed, while also guiding breeders in their pursuit of excellence.

Preserving Heritage and Distinctiveness

Breed standards are the cornerstone of maintaining the distinct genetic lineages that have shaped each breed over centuries. By establishing specific criteria for appearance, temperament, and health, breed standards safeguard the breed's unique identity and prevent the loss of valuable genetic diversity. This meticulous preservation ensures that future generations can appreciate the distinctive traits that have made each breed so cherished.

Ensuring Predictability and Consistency

Breed standards provide breeders with a clear roadmap for producing dogs that are consistent in their physical and behavioral attributes. This consistency is crucial for breeders who seek to maintain the breed's reputation for specific traits, such as working ability, companionship, or athleticism. By adhering to the breed standard, breeders can confidently predict the outcomes of their breeding programs, ensuring that puppies inherit the desired characteristics that have endeared the breed to its enthusiasts.

Protecting Health and Well-being

Breed standards also play a vital role in protecting the health and well-being of purebred dogs. By incorporating health considerations into the standard, breeders can prioritize the prevention and reduction of inherited disorders. For example, certain breeds may be prone to specific joint conditions or eye diseases. The breed standard can mandate screening for these conditions, ensuring that only healthy individuals are used for breeding, thereby reducing the prevalence of such ailments in future generations.

Facilitating Communication and Understanding

Breed standards serve as a common language among breeders, judges, and enthusiasts alike. They provide a clear and concise reference point for discussing and evaluating dogs, fostering a shared understanding of the breed's ideal characteristics. This shared vocabulary facilitates communication and collaboration within the dog breeding community, promoting a collective effort to maintain and improve the breed.

Guiding Ethical Breeding Practices

Breed standards guide breeders toward ethical and

responsible breeding practices. By adhering to the standard, breeders are less likely to engage in practices that compromise the breed's health or temperament. The breed standard acts as a compass, ensuring that breeders prioritize the well-being and longevity of their dogs above all else.

Conclusion

Breed standards are the backbone of purebred dog breeding, providing a vital framework for preserving the unique heritage, ensuring predictability, safeguarding health, facilitating communication, and guiding ethical practices. By adhering to breed standards, breeders play a crucial role in maintaining the integrity and diversity of purebred dogs, ensuring that future generations can continue to appreciate the remarkable qualities that have made each breed so beloved.

22 Identifying Desirable Traits in Different Breeds

In the tapestry of dog breeds, each thread represents a unique combination of physical and behavioral characteristics, meticulously crafted through generations of selective breeding. Identifying desirable traits in different breeds is paramount for responsible dog ownership, ensuring a harmonious coexistence between canine companion and human guardian.

Physical Traits:

Size: Consider your lifestyle and living space. Giant breeds require ample room and exercise, while toy breeds are well-suited for apartment living.

Coat: Factor in grooming needs. Long-haired breeds require regular brushing, while short-haired breeds have lower maintenance requirements.

Color and Markings: While personal preferences vary, certain colors or patterns may be associated with specific health conditions. For instance, white or light-colored breeds may be prone to skin cancer.

Health Considerations: Research common health issues associated with different breeds. Be prepared for potential veterinary expenses and specialized care.

Behavioral Traits:

Temperament: Determine the breed's innate personality. Some breeds are known for their gentleness, while others may possess protective or independent streaks.

Activity Level: Consider your energy levels. High-energy breeds require plenty of exercise and mental stimulation, while low-energy breeds are content with leisurely walks.

Trainability: Assess the breed's learning capacity and responsiveness to training. This factor can influence the ease of establishing desired behaviors.

Socialization: Determine the breed's compatibility with other pets and children. Some breeds are highly sociable, while others may require careful introductions.

Matching Breed Traits to Owner Needs:

To make an informed decision, carefully evaluate your own lifestyle, personality, and circumstances. Consider the following:

Activity Level: Do you enjoy outdoor adventures or prefer a more relaxed lifestyle.

Home Environment: Is your home suitable for a large breed

or more appropriate for a petite companion.

Family Situation: Do you have children or other pets. Choose a breed that is compatible with your family's dynamics.

Health Considerations: Are you prepared to handle potential health concerns associated with specific breeds.

Grooming Needs: Consider the time and effort required to maintain the breed's coat.

Additional Considerations:

Reputable Breeders: Obtain your dog from a responsible breeder who prioritizes health, temperament, and socialization.

Professional Guidance: Consult with a veterinarian or certified dog trainer to gain insights into specific breed characteristics and training requirements.

Socialization and Training: Provide ample opportunities for socialization and training to ensure a well-rounded and well-behaved canine companion. By carefully assessing physical and behavioral characteristics, and matching them to your own needs, you can create a harmonious bond with your canine best friend. Remember, every breed has its unique charm and potential, and the perfect match lies in finding the one that resonates most deeply with your heart and soul.

23 Recognizing Common Genetic Variations in Rabbit Breeds

It is the foundation of genetic diversity, which is essential for the survival and adaptation of populations. In rabbits, genetic variation is responsible for the wide range of breeds and varieties that we see today, each with its own unique characteristics.

Types of Genetic Variation

Genetic variation can occur at different levels, from single nucleotide polymorphisms (SNPs) to large-scale chromosomal rearrangements. SNPs are the most common type of genetic variation, and they can occur throughout the genome. Chromosomal rearrangements, such as deletions, duplications, and inversions, are less common, but they can have a significant impact on the phenotype of an individual.

Common Genetic Variations in Rabbit Breeds

Some of the most common genetic variations in rabbit breeds include:

Coat color: Coat color is one of the most variable traits in rabbits, and it is controlled by a number of different genes. The most common coat colors in rabbits are black, brown, white, and red.
Ear shape: Ear shape is another variable trait in rabbits, and it is controlled by a single gene. The most common ear shapes in rabbits are lop, erect, and semi-erect.
Body size: Body size is a complex trait that is controlled by a number of different genes. The most common body sizes in rabbits are small, medium, and large.
Temperament: Temperament is a behavioral trait that is influenced by both genetics and environment. The most common temperaments in rabbits are friendly, docile, and aggressive.

Importance of Genetic Variation

Genetic variation is important for a number of reasons. First, it provides the raw material for evolution. Without genetic variation, populations would not be able to adapt to changing environmental conditions. Second, genetic variation provides the basis for selective breeding. By selecting for specific traits, breeders can create new breeds of rabbits that are better suited to their needs. Third, genetic variation helps to maintain the health and vitality of populations. By having a diverse gene pool, populations are less likely to be affected by genetic disorders.

Conclusion

Genetic variation is an essential part of the biology of rabbits. It is responsible for the wide range of breeds and varieties that we see today, and it plays an important role in the evolution, adaptation, and health of rabbit populations.

24 Using Breed Information for Successful Breeding Programs

In the realm of animal breeding, harnessing the wealth of breed information available is pivotal to achieving successful breeding programs. Breed information provides a comprehensive understanding of a particular breed's unique characteristics, strengths, and weaknesses, allowing breeders to make informed decisions that optimize the genetic potential of their stock.

Understanding Breed Standards and Characteristics

Breed standards define the ideal physical and behavioral traits that distinguish one breed from another. These standards are meticulously established by breed clubs and organizations based on years of selective breeding and observation. By adhering to breed standards, breeders can ensure that their animals conform to the desired type and maintain the breed's distinctive identity.

In addition to breed standards, breeders should also be familiar with the general characteristics of the breeds they work with. This includes their temperament, health predispositions, performance abilities, and adaptability to different environments. A thorough understanding of breed characteristics allows breeders to select breeding stock that aligns with their specific breeding goals.

Leveraging Genetic Information

Advances in genetic testing have revolutionized the field of animal breeding. Breeders can now utilize DNA analysis to assess the genetic makeup of their animals and make informed decisions about breeding pairs. Genetic testing can identify genetic disorders, predict performance traits, and determine genetic diversity within a breed.

By using genetic information, breeders can avoid breeding animals that carry undesirable traits or genetic diseases. They can also identify animals that possess superior genetic potential for specific traits, such as growth rate, milk production, or athletic ability. This allows them to selectively breed for these desirable traits, improving the overall genetic quality of their stock.

Maintaining Genetic Diversity

Genetic diversity is essential for the long-term health and viability of any breed. A lack of genetic diversity can lead to inbreeding, which increases the risk of genetic disorders and reduces overall fitness. Breeders must take steps to maintain genetic diversity within their breeding programs.

One strategy for maintaining genetic diversity is to introduce new bloodlines into the breeding population. This can be achieved through the acquisition of unrelated animals from other breeding programs or through the use of semen or embryos from animals with different genetic backgrounds.

Another approach to preserving genetic diversity is to avoid excessive inbreeding. Breeders should carefully consider the genetic relationships between breeding pairs and strive to minimize the frequency of closely related matings.

Balancing Breed Standards and Genetic Diversity

Maintaining breed standards while preserving genetic diversity can be a delicate balancing act. Breeders must carefully consider the trade-offs between adhering to breed standards and introducing new genetic material.

In some cases, it may be necessary to deviate slightly from breed standards to maintain genetic diversity. For example, breeders may choose to breed animals with a slightly different color or pattern if they possess superior genetic qualities in other areas.

By carefully weighing the benefits of breed standards against the importance of genetic diversity, breeders can create breeding programs that maintain the breed's unique identity while ensuring its long-term health and viability.

Incorporating Breed Information into Breeding Programs

Integrating breed information into breeding programs is a

comprehensive process that requires a deep understanding of the breed, its genetic characteristics, and the principles of genetic selection. Breeders should develop a clear breeding plan that outlines their goals, breeding strategies, and selection criteria.

The breeding plan should be tailored to the specific breed and the breeder's objectives. It should consider breed standards, genetic diversity, and performance traits. By implementing a well-structured breeding plan, breeders can maximize the genetic potential of their stock and achieve their breeding goals.

Conclusion

Utilizing breed information is a cornerstone of successful breeding programs. By understanding breed standards, leveraging genetic information, maintaining genetic diversity, and incorporating breed information into their breeding plans, breeders can make informed decisions that optimize the genetic potential of their stock. This leads to improved animal health, performance, and the preservation of valuable breed characteristics for future generations.

Chapter 3: The Basics of Rabbit Reproduction

31 Understanding the Rabbit Reproductive Cycle

Understanding the reproductive cycle is crucial for successful breeding, management, and preventing unwanted litters. This comprehensive guide will delve into the intricacies of the rabbit reproductive cycle, providing a thorough understanding of its stages, hormonal regulation, and practical implications.

Stages of the Rabbit Reproductive Cycle

The rabbit reproductive cycle can be divided into four distinct stages:

1. Proestrus (4-5 days): The onset of proestrus is marked by elevated levels of estrogen. The doe's vulva becomes swollen and pink, indicating receptivity to mating. During this stage, the doe is actively seeking a mate and will readily accept copulation.

2. Estrus (1-2 days): Estrus is the period of peak fertility when ovulation occurs. The doe's vulva remains swollen and congested, and she exhibits a lordosis posture when approached by a buck. Copulation during estrus typically results in successful fertilization.

3. Metestrus (10-14 days): After ovulation, the levels of progesterone rise, leading to the formation of the corpus luteum. The corpus luteum secretes progesterone, which maintains the pregnancy if fertilization has occurred. If fertilization does not occur, the corpus luteum regresses, and the cycle resets.

4. Diestrus (9-10 days): Diestrus is the period of inactivity in the reproductive cycle. The vulva returns to its normal size, and the doe is not receptive to mating. The corpus luteum remains active during diestrus, ensuring the continuation of pregnancy if fertilization has occurred.

Hormonal Regulation

The rabbit reproductive cycle is primarily regulated by the hormones estrogen, progesterone, and luteinizing hormone (LH). Estrogen, produced by the ovaries, triggers the onset of proestrus and stimulates the development of the reproductive tract. Progesterone, also produced by the ovaries, maintains pregnancy and inhibits the development of new follicles. LH, produced by the pituitary gland, triggers ovulation and the formation of the corpus luteum.

Practical Implications

Understanding the rabbit reproductive cycle has several practical implications for rabbit owners and breeders:

1. Breeding Management: By monitoring the doe's reproductive cycle, breeders can determine the optimal time for mating to ensure successful fertilization.

2. Litter Planning: Knowing the duration of each stage of the

cycle allows breeders to plan litter sizes and schedules.

3. Preventing Unwanted Litters: Spaying or neutering rabbits can effectively prevent unwanted litters by eliminating the ability to reproduce.

4. Health Monitoring: Reproductive abnormalities, such as prolonged estrus or persistent corpus luteum, can indicate underlying health issues that require veterinary attention.

5. Doe Management: During pregnancy and lactation, does require increased nutrition and care to support their growing litter.

Additional Considerations

Rabbits are induced ovulators, meaning ovulation is triggered by copulation.
The gestation period for rabbits is approximately 31 days.
Litter sizes typically range from 4 to 12 kits.
Does can experience multiple litters per year under optimal conditions.

Conclusion

Understanding the rabbit reproductive cycle is essential for the responsible breeding and management of rabbits. By delving into the stages, hormonal regulation, and practical implications, rabbit owners and breeders can effectively manage their rabbitries, prevent unwanted litters, and ensure the well-being of their animals.

32 Determining Sex in Rabbits

Accurate sex determination allows rabbit owners to make informed decisions regarding breeding, housing, and veterinary care. While rabbits exhibit certain physical characteristics that may suggest their sex, definitive identification requires a thorough examination of specific anatomical features.

Physical Examination

The most reliable method for determining the sex of rabbits is through a physical examination. This involves gently restraining the rabbit and observing the area around the genitals. The following anatomical features are used to differentiate between male and female rabbits:

Male Rabbits (Bucks)

Penis: Bucks have a prominent penis that is typically visible when they are relaxed or urinating. The penis is located on the ventral surface of the body, just behind the navel.
Scrotum: Bucks have a scrotum, which contains the testicles. The scrotum is located just behind the penis and may be visible as two small bulges.
Urogenital Opening: The urogenital opening in bucks is a single hole located on the ventral surface of the body, just behind the penis. Urine and semen are both expelled through this opening.

Female Rabbits (Does)

Vulva: Does have a vulva, which is a small, triangular opening located on the ventral surface of the body, just behind the navel. The vulva may be slightly swollen and pink in sexually mature does.
Urogenital Opening: Does have a urogenital opening located

within the vulva. Urine and feces are both expelled through this opening.

Cervix: The cervix is a small, fleshy protrusion located within the vulva. The cervix is only visible during certain stages of the estrous cycle.

Behavioral Differences

In addition to physical characteristics, certain behavioral differences may also suggest the sex of rabbits. Bucks tend to be more territorial and aggressive than does, especially during the breeding season. They may also exhibit mounting behavior towards other rabbits or objects. Does, on the other hand, are typically more docile and submissive. They may also exhibit nesting behavior when they are preparing to give birth.

Age Considerations

It is important to note that determining the sex of rabbits can be challenging in young rabbits. The anatomical features used for identification may not be fully developed until the rabbits reach sexual maturity, which typically occurs around 4-6 months of age. For young rabbits, it is best to consult with a veterinarian or experienced rabbit breeder for accurate sex determination.

Importance of Accurate Sex Determination

Accurately determining the sex of rabbits is essential for several reasons:

Breeding: Knowing the sex of rabbits is crucial for successful breeding programs. It ensures that only compatible pairs of rabbits are bred together to avoid unwanted litters.

Housing: Male and female rabbits should be housed separately to prevent unwanted pregnancies and aggression.
Veterinary Care: Proper veterinary care requires knowing the sex of rabbits as certain health conditions may be more prevalent in one sex than the other.
General Knowledge: Understanding the sex of rabbits provides valuable information about their behavior, reproductive cycles, and overall well-being.

Conclusion

Determining the sex of rabbits is a fundamental aspect of rabbit ownership and husbandry. By carefully observing the physical characteristics and behavioral differences of rabbits, owners can accurately identify their sex. Accurate sex determination is essential for responsible breeding, appropriate housing, timely veterinary care, and a comprehensive understanding of rabbit behavior and biology.

33 Factors Affecting Reproduction: Age, Health, Nutrition

Age is one of the most important factors affecting reproduction. In women, fertility declines with age, starting in the late 20s and declining more rapidly after age 35. This is due to a number of factors, including:

Decreased ovarian reserve: The number of eggs in the ovaries decreases with age. This is a natural process that begins in utero and continues throughout a woman's life. By the time a woman reaches menopause, she will have lost all of her eggs.
Decreased egg quality: The quality of eggs also declines with

age. This is due to a number of factors, including oxidative damage and chromosomal abnormalities. As a result, older women are more likely to have miscarriages and birth defects.

Changes in the uterus: The uterus also changes with age. The uterine lining becomes thinner and less receptive to implantation. This can make it more difficult for a woman to get pregnant and stay pregnant.

In men, fertility also declines with age, but not as dramatically as in women. Men can father children well into their 60s and 70s, although the risk of birth defects increases with age.

3. 3. 2 Health

A woman's overall health can also affect her fertility. Certain medical conditions, such as obesity, diabetes, and thyroid disease, can make it more difficult to get pregnant and stay pregnant.

Obesity: Obesity is associated with a number of fertility problems, including irregular ovulation, anovulation, and polycystic ovary syndrome (PCOS).

Diabetes: Diabetes can damage the blood vessels and nerves that supply the reproductive organs. This can lead to problems with ovulation, erectile dysfunction, and low sperm count.

Thyroid disease: Thyroid disease can affect the production of hormones that are essential for fertility. This can lead to problems with ovulation, menstrual cycles, and sperm production.

In men, certain medical conditions, such as erectile dysfunction, low sperm count, and testicular cancer, can also affect fertility.

3. 3. 3 Nutrition

A woman's diet can also affect her fertility. Eating a healthy diet that is rich in fruits, vegetables, and whole grains can help to improve fertility. Certain nutrients, such as folic acid, iron, and zinc, are essential for fertility.

Folic acid: Folic acid is a B vitamin that is essential for the prevention of neural tube defects. It is also important for fertility. Women who are trying to conceive should take a folic acid supplement of at least 400 mcg per day.
Iron: Iron is a mineral that is essential for the production of red blood cells. Women who are deficient in iron may have difficulty getting pregnant and staying pregnant.
Zinc: Zinc is a mineral that is essential for the production of sperm. Men who are deficient in zinc may have low sperm count and fertility problems.

Eating a healthy diet can help to improve fertility in both men and women.

Conclusion

Age, health, and nutrition are all important factors that can affect reproduction. By understanding the effects of these factors, you can take steps to improve your fertility and increase your chances of having a healthy baby.

34 Successful Mating Techniques for Optimal Results

In the realm of animal breeding, achieving successful mating is paramount for ensuring genetic diversity, maintaining breed standards, and maximizing reproductive efficiency. Employing the appropriate mating techniques can significantly enhance the probability of achieving optimal results, producing healthy offspring with desirable traits.

Selection of Breeding Stock

The cornerstone of successful mating lies in the judicious selection of breeding stock. This entails evaluating the genetic makeup, physical attributes, and overall health of potential mates. Identifying animals with complementary traits, such as desired coat color, size, or temperament, increases the likelihood of producing offspring that embody these sought-after characteristics.

Control over Mating

Mating can be controlled through various methods, each with its own advantages and disadvantages. Natural mating, where animals are allowed to mate freely, is suitable for smaller populations and situations where genetic control is less stringent. However, this method can lead to inbreeding and unpredictable outcomes.

Artificial insemination (AI) offers greater control over mating and allows for the utilization of superior sires to improve the genetic makeup of offspring. This technique involves collecting semen from a selected male and introducing it into the reproductive tract of the female at the optimal time for conception. AI facilitates selective breeding, reduces the risk of disease transmission, and enables the use of frozen or chilled semen, allowing for greater flexibility in breeding programs.

Timing of Mating

The timing of mating is critical for achieving optimal results. Identifying the female's estrous cycle, the period of sexual receptivity, is essential. Various methods, such as observing behavioral cues or using hormonal assays, can be employed to determine the optimal time for mating. By aligning mating with the female's ovulation, the chances of successful fertilization are increased.

Environmental Factors

Environmental factors can significantly impact the success of mating. Providing a stress-free and conducive environment is crucial. Adequate nutrition, housing, and social interactions contribute to the overall health and reproductive capacity of breeding animals. Additionally, maintaining optimal temperature and lighting conditions can enhance breeding success.

Monitoring and Intervention

Regular monitoring of the mating process is essential to identify any potential issues and intervene accordingly. Close observation of mating behavior, including mounting, copulation, and ejaculation, can provide valuable insights into the effectiveness of the mating. If difficulties arise, such as reluctance to mate or unsuccessful fertilization, prompt intervention may be necessary. Veterinary assistance, hormonal treatments, or adjustments to the breeding environment can help overcome challenges and improve mating outcomes.

Record Keeping and Evaluation

Accurate record keeping is essential for evaluating the success of mating techniques and making informed decisions for future breeding programs. This includes documenting the mating dates, breeding pairs, any interventions performed, and the resulting offspring. By analyzing these records, breeders can identify patterns, assess the effectiveness of different mating techniques, and fine-tune their strategies for continuous improvement.

Conclusion

Successful mating techniques are an integral aspect of animal breeding, enabling the production of healthy and desirable offspring. By selecting suitable breeding stock, controlling mating through appropriate methods, timing mating optimally, considering environmental factors, monitoring the process, and maintaining accurate records, breeders can significantly enhance their chances of achieving optimal results. Through continued research and advancements in breeding techniques, the field of animal breeding continues to evolve, ensuring the preservation and improvement of our valuable animal resources.

Chapter 4: Mendelian Inheritance in Rabbits

41 Dominant and Recessive Alleles

Gregor Mendel's Experiments: Unveiling the Foundation of Inheritance

The field of genetics owes its genesis to the groundbreaking work of Gregor Mendel, an Austrian monk and scientist, who conducted meticulous experiments with pea plants in the mid-1800s. Through his meticulous observations and mathematical analysis, Mendel elucidated the fundamental principles of heredity, laying the groundwork for our understanding of the transmission of traits from one generation to the next.

The Concept of Alleles: Variations in Genetic Material

At the core of Mendel's discoveries lies the concept of alleles, alternative forms of a gene that occupy a specific locus on a chromosome. Each gene, residing at a specific location along the chromosome, exists in various forms, each representing a distinct allele. These variations arise from slight alterations in the DNA sequence of the gene, resulting in different versions of the encoded protein or RNA molecule.

Dominance and Recessiveness: A Tale of Allelic Expression

When an individual inherits two different alleles for a particular gene, one from each parent, the expression of these alleles determines the observable trait. In such cases, one allele may exhibit dominance over the other, resulting in the dominant phenotype being expressed in the individual. The allele that remains masked, failing to manifest its effects, is termed the recessive allele.

Homozygous and Heterozygous Genotypes

The genetic makeup of an individual, with respect to a particular gene, is referred to as its genotype. An individual is homozygous for a gene if they inherit identical alleles from both parents. Conversely, if an individual inherits different alleles for a gene, they are considered heterozygous.

Dominant and Recessive Phenotypes

The observable expression of a gene, whether dominant or recessive, is known as the phenotype. When an individual is homozygous for a dominant allele, the dominant phenotype is expressed. In the case of a homozygous recessive genotype, the recessive phenotype is observed. However, when an individual is heterozygous, carrying both dominant and recessive alleles, the dominant allele prevails, and the dominant phenotype is expressed.

Punnett Squares: A Tool for Predicting Inheritance Patterns

Punnett squares, named after the British geneticist Reginald Punnett, are valuable tools employed to predict the potential outcomes of genetic crosses. These diagrams depict the possible combinations of alleles that can be inherited from each parent, allowing researchers to calculate the probability of specific phenotypes appearing in the offspring.

Applications of Dominant and Recessive Alleles

The principles governing dominant and recessive alleles have far-reaching implications in various fields, including medicine, agriculture, and conservation biology. In medicine, understanding dominant and recessive traits aids in diagnosing genetic disorders and predicting disease susceptibility. In agriculture, dominant traits can be selectively bred to enhance crop yield and resistance to pests or diseases. In conservation biology, identifying dominant and recessive alleles is crucial for preserving genetic diversity and mitigating the impact of genetic drift within endangered species.

Examples of Dominant and Recessive Traits in Humans

Numerous human traits exhibit dominant and recessive inheritance patterns. Some well-known examples include:

- Dominant: Brown eye color, attached earlobes, dimples
- Recessive: Blue eye color, free earlobes, cystic fibrosis, sickle cell anemia

Conclusion

The concepts of dominant and recessive alleles, first elucidated by Gregor Mendel, represent a cornerstone of genetics. These principles govern the inheritance of traits and provide a framework for understanding the diversity of life. From the intricate workings of human genetics to the preservation of endangered species, the principles of dominance and recessiveness continue to shape our understanding of the living world.

42 Punnett Squares: Predicting Offspring Genotypes and Phenotypes

In the realm of genetics, Punnett squares serve as invaluable tools for predicting the possible genotypes and phenotypes of offspring. Introduced by the renowned geneticist Reginald Punnett, these visual representations provide a systematic and accessible approach to understanding inheritance patterns. Punnett squares are particularly useful for analyzing monohybrid crosses, where parents differ in only one gene of interest.

Understanding Genotypes and Phenotypes

To fully appreciate the significance of Punnett squares, it is essential to understand the fundamental concepts of genotypes and phenotypes. A genotype refers to the genetic makeup of an organism, consisting of the specific alleles (alternative forms of a gene) present at a particular gene locus. In contrast, a phenotype describes the observable characteristics or traits exhibited by an organism, which are influenced by both genetic and environmental factors.

Constructing a Punnett Square

Creating a Punnett square involves several key steps:

1. Identify the parental genotypes: Determine the alleles present in the gametes (sex cells) of each parent.
2. Draw a square with four boxes: Each box represents a possible combination of alleles in the offspring.
3. Label the rows and columns: Label the rows with the maternal gametes (one allele per row) and the columns with the paternal gametes (one allele per column).

4. Fill in the boxes: Each box is filled with the combination of alleles inherited from the corresponding row and column.

Predicting Genotypes

By analyzing the Punnett square, we can determine the possible genotypes of the offspring. The alleles inherited from each parent combine in different combinations, leading to distinct genotypic outcomes. For instance, if one parent has a dominant allele (A) and a recessive allele (a), and the other parent has two recessive alleles (aa), the Punnett square would predict a 50% chance of heterozygous (Aa) offspring and a 50% chance of homozygous recessive (aa) offspring.

Predicting Phenotypes

The phenotypes of offspring can also be predicted using Punnett squares, based on the concept of dominant and recessive alleles. A dominant allele masks the expression of a recessive allele when both are present. If a dominant allele is inherited from either parent, the offspring will exhibit the dominant phenotype. Conversely, if only recessive alleles are inherited, the offspring will exhibit the recessive phenotype.

Limitations of Punnett Squares

While Punnett squares provide valuable insights into inheritance patterns, they do have certain limitations. They:

Assume that alleles segregate independently during gamete formation (not always true for linked genes).
Do not account for the influence of environmental factors on phenotype.

Predict probabilities rather than absolute outcomes.

Applications of Punnett Squares

Punnett squares find numerous applications in genetics, including:

Predicting offspring traits in selective breeding programs.
Studying inheritance patterns in human pedigrees.
Understanding genetic disorders and their inheritance patterns.
Teaching and visualizing basic principles of Mendelian genetics.

Conclusion

Punnett squares are a fundamental tool in genetics, enabling us to predict the possible genotypes and phenotypes of offspring. By understanding the principles of inheritance and applying Punnett squares, we can gain a deeper appreciation for the intricate mechanisms that govern the transmission of genetic traits.

43 Examples of Mendelian Traits in Rabbits: Coat Color, Fur Type

Gregor Mendel's pioneering work with pea plants laid the foundation for our understanding of the inheritance of traits. His principles of segregation and independent assortment have been instrumental in unraveling the genetic basis of many characteristics in a wide range of organisms, including rabbits. In this section, we will explore two classic Mendelian traits in rabbits: coat color and fur type, and trace their inheritance patterns according to Mendelian principles.

4. 3. 1 Coat Color

Coat color is a highly visible and easily recognizable trait in rabbits, and its inheritance follows Mendelian principles. The agouti gene, denoted by A, is responsible for producing the characteristic banded pattern of hairs, resulting in a coat with alternating dark and light bands. The recessive allele, a, leads to a solid coat color, lacking the banded pattern.

When a homozygous dominant rabbit (AA) is crossed with a homozygous recessive rabbit (aa), all the offspring will be heterozygous (Aa) and will exhibit the agouti pattern. This demonstrates the dominance of the A allele over the a allele.

In a cross between two heterozygous rabbits (Aa x Aa), the offspring will exhibit a 3:1 ratio of agouti to solid-colored rabbits. This is because the A allele has a 75% chance of being passed on to offspring, while the a allele has a 25% chance. The resulting genotypic ratio is 1 AA : 2 Aa : 1 aa, which translates to a phenotypic ratio of 3 agouti : 1 solid-colored.

4. 3. 2 Fur Type

Another Mendelian trait in rabbits is fur type, which can be either normal (straight) or rex (curly). The rex gene, denoted by R, is responsible for the curly fur phenotype. The dominant allele, R, leads to straight fur, while the recessive allele, r, results in curly fur.

When a homozygous dominant rabbit (RR) is crossed with a homozygous recessive rabbit (rr), all the offspring will be heterozygous (Rr) and will have straight fur. This again demonstrates the dominance of the R allele over the r allele.

In a cross between two heterozygous rabbits (Rr x Rr), the offspring will exhibit a 3:1 ratio of straight-haired to curly-haired rabbits. This follows the same principle as in coat color inheritance, where the dominant allele has a 75% chance of being passed on to offspring, while the recessive allele has a 25% chance. The resulting genotypic ratio is 1 RR : 2 Rr : 1 rr, which translates to a phenotypic ratio of 3 straight-haired : 1 curly-haired.

4. 3. 3 Conclusion

The inheritance patterns of coat color and fur type in rabbits provide clear examples of Mendelian traits. These traits are governed by single genes with dominant and recessive alleles, and their inheritance follows the principles of segregation and independent assortment. Understanding these basic principles of genetics is essential for comprehending the inheritance of more complex traits and for unraveling the genetic basis of various traits in different organisms.

44 Understanding the Concept of Heterozygosity and Homozygosity

These concepts are crucial for understanding the inheritance patterns of traits and the genetic diversity within populations.

Heterozygosity: A Symphony of Genetic Diversity

Heterozygosity refers to the condition where an individual possesses two different alleles for a particular gene. Alleles are alternative forms of a gene that occupy the same locus on a chromosome. In a heterozygous individual, the two alleles are inherited from different parents. The presence of different alleles provides genetic variability, allowing for a wider range of phenotypic expression within a population.

Homozygosity: Harmony in Genetic Similarity

Homozygosity, on the other hand, occurs when an individual possesses two identical alleles for a particular gene. Both alleles are inherited from the same parent. Homozygosity can result from self-fertilization in plants or mating between closely related individuals. It reduces genetic diversity and can lead to the expression of recessive traits that may otherwise remain hidden in heterozygous individuals.

The Significance of Heterozygosity

Heterozygosity has several important implications for individuals and populations. First, it provides a level of genetic diversity that enhances the adaptability of a population to changing environmental conditions. Individuals with different genetic backgrounds may respond differently to environmental pressures, increasing the overall resilience of the population.

Second, heterozygosity can mask the expression of recessive alleles. Recessive alleles are only expressed in homozygous individuals, where both copies of the gene carry the recessive trait. In heterozygous individuals, the dominant allele masks the expression of the recessive allele, preventing it from manifesting in the phenotype.

The Role of Homozygosity

While heterozygosity promotes genetic diversity, homozygosity also plays an essential role in certain genetic processes. For instance, homozygous individuals can express both dominant and recessive traits, providing a clearer understanding of the underlying genetic makeup of an individual.

Homozygosity can also lead to the development of genetic disorders. Recessive genetic disorders are only expressed in homozygous individuals, making homozygosity an important consideration in genetic counseling and the prevention of inherited diseases.

Implications for Conservation

In conservation biology, maintaining genetic diversity is crucial for the long-term survival of species. Heterozygosity helps preserve genetic diversity within populations, reducing the risk of extinction due to genetic uniformity. Conservation efforts often focus on maintaining heterozygosity and preventing the loss of genetic variation.

Conclusion

Heterozygosity and homozygosity are fundamental concepts in genetics that describe the genetic makeup of individuals and populations. Heterozygosity promotes genetic diversity and enhances adaptability, while homozygosity can reveal recessive traits and contribute to genetic disorders. Understanding these concepts is essential for comprehending inheritance patterns, predicting phenotypic outcomes, and implementing effective conservation strategies.

Chapter 5: Beyond Mendelian Inheritance: Complex Genetic Traits

51 Polygenic Traits: Multiple Genes Influencing a Trait

In the realm of genetics, the relationship between genes and traits is often portrayed as a straightforward one-to-one correspondence. However, this simplistic view belies the intricate complexities that underlie the inheritance of many human characteristics. A substantial proportion of our traits, including those that shape our physical appearance, behavior, and susceptibility to diseases, are not governed by a single gene but rather by the combined effects of multiple genes. These traits are known as polygenic traits.

The concept of polygenic inheritance emerged from the realization that many traits exhibit continuous variation within a population. For instance, consider the height of humans. Height is not a binary characteristic; it exists along a spectrum, with individuals ranging from short to tall. This continuous variation suggests that height is not determined by a single gene with two distinct alleles, but rather by a combination of genetic and environmental factors.

Multiple Genes, Additive Effects

At the molecular level, polygenic traits are influenced by the additive effects of multiple genes, each contributing a small increment to the overall trait value. These genes may be located on different chromosomes or on the same chromosome but at different loci. The cumulative effect of these genetic variations results in a distribution of trait values that typically follows a bell curve, with most individuals clustering around an average value and fewer individuals falling at the extremes.

Complex Interactions

While the concept of additive effects provides a foundational understanding of polygenic inheritance, it is important to recognize that the genetic architecture underlying polygenic traits is often far more complex. Genes do not operate in isolation; they interact with each other and with the environment, giving rise to intricate genetic networks that shape our traits.

These interactions can be classified into two broad categories:

1. Epistasis: Epistasis occurs when the effect of one gene is modified by the presence or absence of another gene. For example, the expression of a gene involved in hair color may be influenced by the presence of a gene that regulates hair texture.

2. Pleiotropy: Pleiotropy occurs when a single gene influences multiple traits. For instance, a gene involved in regulating blood pressure may also affect kidney function.

Environmental Influences

In addition to genetic factors, environmental factors also play a significant role in shaping polygenic traits. Environmental exposures, such as nutrition, stress, and exposure to toxins, can influence gene expression and modify trait values. The interplay between genetics and environment is particularly evident in complex diseases, where both genetic predisposition and environmental factors contribute to disease risk.

Implications for Health and Medicine

The understanding of polygenic inheritance has profound implications for health and medicine. Many common diseases, including heart disease, diabetes, and cancer, are polygenic in nature. By identifying the genetic variants that contribute to these diseases, researchers can develop more targeted therapies and personalized approaches to disease prevention and treatment.

Furthermore, polygenic risk scores, which estimate an individual's likelihood of developing a particular disease based on their genetic profile, have the potential to revolutionize healthcare by enabling early detection, preventive measures, and tailored treatment plans.

Conclusion

Polygenic traits, influenced by the combined effects of multiple genes and environmental factors, represent a fundamental aspect of human inheritance. The study of polygenic traits offers a deeper understanding of the complex interplay between genetics, environment, and our health. As we continue to unravel the genetic architecture of these traits, we gain valuable insights into the etiology of diseases and the development of more effective therapeutic strategies.

52 Epistasis: Interaction Between Different Genes

In the realm of genetics, the interaction between different genes, known as epistasis, plays a significant role in shaping the inheritance of traits. Epistasis refers to the phenomenon where the effect of one gene is influenced or modified by the presence of another gene. This interaction can lead to a departure from the expected Mendelian inheritance patterns.

Types of Epistasis

Epistasis can manifest in various forms, each with distinct consequences on trait inheritance:

Dominant Epistasis: In this type of epistasis, a dominant allele at one locus masks the expression of alleles at a different locus. For instance, in pea plants, the gene for flower color exhibits dominant epistasis. The presence of a dominant allele for purple flowers (P) will override the expression of an allele for white flowers (p), even if the latter is present in the genotype.

Recessive Epistasis: In contrast to dominant epistasis, recessive epistasis occurs when a recessive allele at one locus suppresses the expression of alleles at another locus. An example of recessive epistasis can be observed in mice. The coat color of mice is controlled by two genes: one for black (B) and the other for brown (b). However, a recessive allele at a third locus, known as the albino locus (a), inhibits the expression of both black and brown alleles, resulting in a white coat color.

Double Recessive Epistasis: This type of epistasis occurs when two recessive alleles at different loci are required to produce a particular phenotype. An example can be seen in the inheritance of albinism in humans. Albinism is caused by mutations in either of two genes involved in melanin production. In order for an individual to exhibit albinism, they must inherit two recessive alleles, one from each gene.

Complementation: Complementation occurs when two or more genes interact to produce a functional phenotype. This phenomenon is often observed in cases where multiple genes are involved in a single metabolic pathway. For instance, in the synthesis of a certain amino acid, two different genes may encode enzymes that catalyze sequential steps in the pathway. If mutations occur in both genes, the pathway is disrupted, leading to an inability to produce the amino acid. However, if each gene is mutated in different individuals and they mate, their offspring may inherit a functional copy of each gene, allowing for the synthesis of the amino acid.

Examples of Epistasis

Numerous examples of epistasis can be found throughout the natural world:

Plant Pigment Synthesis: In plants, the production of pigments like anthocyanins is often controlled by multiple genes that interact epistatically. For example, in snapdragons, one gene determines the presence or absence of red pigment, while a second gene controls the production of purple pigment. The interaction between these genes results in a range of flower colors, from red to purple to white.

Eye Color in Humans: The inheritance of human eye color is a classic example of epistasis. Several genes are involved in determining eye color, but one particularly influential gene is OCA2. Mutations in OCA2 lead to a reduction in melanin production, resulting in lighter eye colors. However, another gene, TYR, also plays a role in melanin production. If an individual inherits a recessive allele of TYR, they will have blue eyes regardless of their OCA2 genotype.

Significance of Epistasis

Epistasis has important implications for both evolutionary biology and human health:

Evolutionary Biology: Epistasis can contribute to the evolution of new traits and the maintenance of genetic diversity. By altering the effects of other genes, epistasis can influence the fitness of individuals in different environments. This can lead to the evolution of new adaptations and the preservation of genetic variation within populations.

Human Health: Epistasis plays a role in the inheritance of complex diseases, such as cancer, cardiovascular disease, and diabetes. By understanding the epistatic interactions between genes, researchers can identify genetic variants that increase the risk of developing certain diseases. This knowledge can lead to the development of personalized medicine approaches that take into account individual genetic profiles. Understanding epistasis is essential for comprehending the inheritance of traits, the evolution of new adaptations, and the genetic basis of complex diseases.

53 Environmental Influences on Genetic Traits

While genes provide the blueprint for an organism's development, environmental factors can influence the way those genes are expressed, leading to phenotypic variation within a population. Environmental influences on genetic traits are a fundamental concept in biology, with implications for understanding human health, disease, and evolution.

Epigenetics and Environmental Influences

Epigenetics refers to changes in gene expression that do not involve alterations in the DNA sequence itself. These changes can be induced by environmental factors and are often heritable across generations. Epigenetic mechanisms include DNA methylation, histone modification, and non-coding RNAs.

DNA Methylation

DNA methylation involves the addition of a methyl group to cytosine nucleotides within DNA. This modification can alter gene expression by affecting the binding of transcription factors to DNA. Environmental factors such as stress, diet, and toxins can influence DNA methylation patterns, leading to changes in gene expression.

Histone Modification

Histones are proteins that package DNA into chromatin. Modifications to histones, such as acetylation and methylation, can alter the accessibility of DNA to transcription factors. These modifications can be influenced by environmental cues, such as nutrient availability and hormonal signals.

Non-Coding RNAs

Non-coding RNAs, such as microRNAs and long non-coding RNAs, can regulate gene expression by binding to messenger RNA (mRNA) and preventing its translation. Environmental factors can influence the expression of non-coding RNAs, thereby altering the expression of their target genes.

Environmental Influences on Human Health and Disease

Environmental influences on genetic traits have profound implications for human health and disease. For instance, exposure to air pollution has been linked to changes in DNA methylation patterns and increased risk of respiratory diseases such as asthma. Similarly, early-life malnutrition can lead to epigenetic changes that increase susceptibility to obesity and metabolic disorders later in life.

Epigenetic Inheritance

Epigenetic changes can be heritable across generations, even in the absence of changes in DNA sequence. This phenomenon, known as epigenetic inheritance, has been observed in both plants and animals. Transgenerational epigenetic inheritance can provide a mechanism for adaptation to changing environmental conditions.

Evolutionary Implications

Environmental influences on genetic traits can also drive evolutionary change. Over time, environmental factors that select for certain genetic variants can lead to changes in the frequency of those variants within a population. This process, known as epigenetics-based evolution, can occur rapidly, allowing populations to adapt to new environmental challenges.

Conclusion

Environmental influences on genetic traits are a complex and dynamic area of research. Epigenetic mechanisms play a critical role in mediating these influences, leading to phenotypic variation and affecting human health and disease. Understanding the interplay between genes and the environment is essential for unraveling the complexities of human biology and developing strategies to mitigate environmental health risks and promote well-being.

54 Examples of Complex Traits in Rabbits: Size, Body Type

Complex traits are influenced by multiple genes and environmental factors and exhibit continuous variation within a population. In rabbits, size and body type are two such complex traits that have been extensively studied. These traits are of considerable economic importance in commercial rabbit production, as they impact meat yield, feed efficiency, and overall health and well-being.

Size

Body size in rabbits is a polygenic trait, meaning it is controlled by the interaction of several genes. These genes influence various aspects of growth and development, including skeletal size, muscle mass, and fat deposition. The heritability of body size in rabbits is moderate to high, indicating that genetic factors play a significant role in its determination.

Environmental factors, such as nutrition, management practices, and disease status, can also impact body size. Optimal nutrition during growth is essential for achieving maximum size potential. Proper management practices, including appropriate housing and exercise, can also promote healthy growth and development. Conversely, poor nutrition, inadequate management, or health problems can lead to stunted growth and reduced body size.

Body Type

Body type in rabbits refers to the overall conformation and shape of the body. It is influenced by both genetic and environmental factors. Several body types have been recognized in rabbits, each with distinct characteristics.

Compact type: Rabbits with a compact body type have a short, broad body with well-developed musculature. They are typically heavier than rabbits with other body types and have a good meat-to-bone ratio.

Semi-compact type: Rabbits with a semi-compact body type are intermediate in size and shape between compact and elongated types. They have a well-proportioned body with good musculature and a moderate meat-to-bone ratio.

Elongated type: Rabbits with an elongated body type have a long, narrow body with less developed musculature. They are typically lighter than rabbits with other body types and have a lower meat-to-bone ratio.

The choice of body type for commercial rabbit production depends on the specific production goals and market demands. Compact and semi-compact rabbits are preferred for meat production due to their higher meat yield and better feed conversion efficiency. Elongated rabbits are often used for fur production or as pets.

Genetic Control of Size and Body Type

The genetic control of size and body type in rabbits is complex, involving the interaction of multiple genes with varying effects. Quantitative trait loci (QTL) studies have identified several genomic regions associated with these traits.

Size: QTLs for body weight have been identified on several chromosomes in rabbits, including chromosomes 1, 2, 3, 4, 7, and 10. These QTLs contain genes involved in growth hormone production, skeletal development, and muscle growth.

Body type: QTLs for body shape and conformation have been identified on chromosomes 2, 3, 5, 7, and 10 in rabbits. These QTLs contain genes involved in skeletal development, muscle distribution, and fat deposition.

Environmental Influences on Size and Body Type

Environmental factors can significantly impact size and body type in rabbits. These factors include:

Nutrition: Optimal nutrition during growth is essential for achieving maximum size potential. A balanced diet, rich in protein, energy, and essential nutrients, is necessary for proper skeletal and muscular development.

Management practices: Proper management practices, including appropriate housing, exercise, and veterinary care, can promote healthy growth and development. Adequate space, fresh air, and opportunities for exercise are essential for rabbits to reach their full size and body type potential.

Health status: Diseases and health problems can negatively impact growth and development in rabbits. Early detection and treatment of diseases can help prevent stunted growth and other adverse effects on size and body type.

Conclusion

Size and body type are complex traits in rabbits, influenced by multiple genes and environmental factors. Understanding the genetic and environmental factors that contribute to these traits is crucial for improving rabbit production and breeding programs. By optimizing nutrition, management practices, and health status, rabbit producers can maximize size and body type to meet specific production goals and market demands.

Chapter 6: Coat Color Genetics

61 Basic Coat Colors in Rabbits

The coat color of rabbits is determined by a complex interaction of multiple genes. The basic coat colors are black, brown, chocolate, and lilac. These colors are produced by the interaction of two genes: the A locus and the B locus.

The A locus has two alleles: A and a. The A allele produces black pigment, while the a allele produces brown pigment. The B locus has two alleles: B and b. The B allele produces chocolate pigment, while the b allele produces lilac pigment.

The interaction of these two genes produces the following coat colors:

Black: AA BB
Brown: Aa BB
Chocolate: AA bb
Lilac: Aa bb

In addition to these basic coat colors, there are a number of other coat colors that can be produced by the interaction of other genes. These colors include:

Blue: aa BB
Gray: aa Bb
Fawn: aa bb
Cream: A- bb

Silver: A- B-

The coat color of rabbits can be affected by a number of environmental factors, such as temperature and diet. For example, rabbits that are exposed to cold temperatures may have a darker coat color than rabbits that are exposed to warm temperatures. Rabbits that are fed a diet that is high in protein may have a lighter coat color than rabbits that are fed a diet that is low in protein.

Inheritance of Coat Color

The inheritance of coat color in rabbits is a simple Mendelian trait. This means that the coat color of a rabbit is determined by the alleles that it inherits from its parents.

If a rabbit inherits two A alleles, it will have a black coat. If a rabbit inherits two a alleles, it will have a brown coat. If a rabbit inherits one A allele and one a allele, it will have a chocolate coat. If a rabbit inherits two B alleles, it will have a chocolate coat. If a rabbit inherits two b alleles, it will have a lilac coat. If a rabbit inherits one B allele and one b allele, it will have a gray coat.

The interaction of these two genes produces the following coat colors:

Black: AA BB
Brown: Aa BB
Chocolate: AA bb
Lilac: Aa bb
Blue: aa BB
Gray: aa Bb
Fawn: aa bb
Cream: A- bb

Silver: A- B-

Coat Color and Rabbit Health

The coat color of a rabbit does not have any impact on its health. However, some coat colors may be more susceptible to certain diseases than others. For example, rabbits with white coats are more susceptible to sunburn than rabbits with darker coats.

Conclusion

The coat color of rabbits is a complex and fascinating trait. The interaction of multiple genes produces a wide variety of coat colors, each with its own unique characteristics. The coat color of a rabbit is a valuable tool for breeders, who can use it to select rabbits for specific breeding programs.

62 Understanding the Agouti Gene and its Variations

The agouti gene is a fascinating locus that plays a pivotal role in determining the coat color of many animals, including mice, rabbits, and humans. Its diverse allelic variants give rise to a wide spectrum of coat patterns and pigmentation, making it an intriguing subject for genetic and evolutionary studies.

The Agouti Protein and Its Function

The agouti gene encodes a protein called agouti signaling protein (ASIP). ASIP acts as a paracrine factor, meaning it is secreted by one cell and affects nearby target cells. In the context of coat color, ASIP primarily targets melanocytes, the cells responsible for producing melanin, the pigment that gives hair and skin its color.

Regulation of Melanin Production

ASIP exerts its influence on melanocytes by modulating the production of melanin. Specifically, ASIP binds to the melanocortin 1 receptor (MC1R) on melanocytes, which is part of the signaling pathway that controls melanin synthesis. When ASIP binds to MC1R, it activates the production of eumelanin, a dark brown or black pigment.

Conversely, in the absence of ASIP binding, MC1R triggers the production of pheomelanin, a reddish-yellow pigment. The ratio of eumelanin to pheomelanin determines the overall coat color of the animal.

Agouti Allelic Variants and Their Impact

The agouti gene exhibits a range of allelic variants, each of which affects ASIP production or function differently. These variations lead to distinct coat color patterns and phenotypes:

Wild-type agouti (A): Produces functional ASIP, resulting in a banded or brindled coat pattern with alternating dark and light bands.

Dominant yellow (A^Y): A loss-of-function mutation that prevents ASIP production, leading to a solid yellow coat color due to the exclusive production of pheomelanin.

Recessive black (a): Another loss-of-function mutation that abolishes ASIP production entirely. This results in a solid black coat color as eumelanin production is uninhibited.

Extreme dominant spotting (A^es): A dominant mutation that produces a coat with large white patches and minimal pigmentation due to disrupted ASIP signaling.

Evolutionary Significance of Agouti Variation

The diversity of agouti alleles has important evolutionary implications. In certain environments, particular coat color patterns may confer selective advantages. For instance, banded agouti patterns provide camouflage in habitats with patchy vegetation, while solid black coats may offer thermal insulation in colder climates.

The existence of multiple agouti alleles allows populations to adapt to changing environmental conditions by selecting for alleles that enhance survival and reproductive success. This genetic flexibility contributes to the adaptability and resilience of many species.

Agouti Gene in Humans

The agouti gene has also been studied in humans, where it is associated with hair color and obesity. Variations in the agouti gene have been linked to red hair, as well as increased risk of obesity and metabolic disorders.

Understanding the agouti gene and its variations provides valuable insights into the genetic basis of coat color and pigmentation in animals, including humans. It highlights the intricate interplay between genes, the environment, and the evolution of diverse phenotypic traits.

63 Pattern Genes: Creating Color Variations

Pattern genes are genetic variations that affect the distribution and intensity of color pigments in animals, plants, and other organisms. These genes control the formation of specific color patterns, markings, and variations within a species, contributing to the diverse array of colors and patterns observed in nature.

How Pattern Genes Work

Pattern genes influence color variations by regulating the expression of pigmentation genes, which produce and deposit color pigments into cells. By controlling the timing, location, and amount of pigment deposition, pattern genes can create intricate and diverse color patterns.

Types of Pattern Genes

Numerous types of pattern genes exist, each with unique effects on color variation. Some of the most common include:

Agouti: Controls the distribution of dark and light pigments, creating banded or ticked patterns.
Tabby: Creates striped or spotted patterns in mammals and fish.
Piebald: Affects the distribution of white markings, resulting in piebald or spotted patterns.
Leucism: Reduces or eliminates all pigmentation, resulting in albino or white coloration.
Melanism: Increases pigmentation, resulting in darker coloration.

Examples of Pattern Genes in Nature

Pattern genes play a crucial role in shaping the diversity of color patterns found in the natural world. For instance, the agouti gene in mice controls the distribution of black and yellow pigments, creating the banded or ticked coat patterns characteristic of wild mice.

In zebrafish, the tabby gene influences the formation of stripes and spots, resulting in the striking color patterns that distinguish different zebrafish species. Similarly, the piebald gene in horses creates the distinctive white markings associated with breeds such as the Appaloosa and Paint Horse.

Genetic Basis of Pattern Variation

Pattern genes are often inherited in a Mendelian manner, with dominant and recessive alleles determining the resulting phenotype. However, the expression of pattern genes can also be influenced by other genetic factors, including modifier genes and environmental factors.

Evolutionary Significance of Pattern Genes

Pattern genes have significant evolutionary implications. Color patterns play important roles in camouflage, mate attraction, species recognition, and predator avoidance. For example, the striped patterns of zebras may help them blend into their surroundings and avoid predators.

Over time, natural selection can favor specific pattern genes that provide an adaptive advantage to individuals within a population. This process can lead to the evolution of distinct color patterns within species and the diversification of colors and patterns across the animal and plant kingdoms.

Conclusion

Pattern genes are fascinating genetic variations that shape the diverse array of color patterns observed in nature. By understanding the mechanisms underlying pattern gene expression, scientists can gain insights into the evolution of color diversity and the complex genetic processes that govern the formation of biological form and function.

64 Common Coat Color Mutations and Their Inheritance

Coat color in dogs is a complex trait that is influenced by multiple genes. The inheritance of coat color can be challenging to understand, but it is important for breeders to have a basic understanding of the genetics involved in order to produce dogs with the desired coat colors.

The Basics of Coat Color Inheritance

The color of a dog's coat is determined by the amount and distribution of two types of pigment: eumelanin (black or brown) and phaeomelanin (red or yellow). The amount and distribution of these pigments is controlled by a number of genes, including the Agouti gene, the Extension gene, and the Melanocortin-1 receptor (MC1R) gene.

The Agouti gene controls the distribution of eumelanin and phaeomelanin. The wild-type Agouti allele (A) produces a banded pattern of eumelanin and phaeomelanin, resulting in a coat color that is known as agouti. The recessive black allele (a) produces a solid black coat color, and the recessive red allele (a^y) produces a solid red coat color.

The Extension gene controls the production of eumelanin. The wild-type Extension allele (E) allows for the production of eumelanin, resulting in a black or brown coat color. The recessive yellow allele (e) inhibits the production of eumelanin, resulting in a yellow or cream coat color.

The MC1R gene controls the production of phaeomelanin. The wild-type MC1R allele (M) allows for the production of phaeomelanin, resulting in a red or yellow coat color. The recessive black allele (m) inhibits the production of phaeomelanin, resulting in a black or brown coat color.

Common Coat Color Mutations

There are a number of common coat color mutations that can occur in dogs. These mutations can result in a wide variety of coat colors, including white, blue, merle, and brindle.

White: The white coat color is caused by a mutation in the SLC45A2 gene. This mutation prevents the production of melanin, resulting in a complete lack of pigmentation in the coat.
Blue: The blue coat color is caused by a mutation in the SLC24A5 gene. This mutation reduces the amount of eumelanin that is produced, resulting in a coat color that is blue or gray.
Merle: The merle coat color is caused by a mutation in the SILV gene. This mutation disrupts the distribution of eumelanin, resulting in a coat color that is characterized by patches of black and gray.
Brindle: The brindle coat color is caused by a mutation in the KRT71 gene. This mutation disrupts the normal growth of hair follicles, resulting in a coat color that is characterized by stripes of black and brown.

Inheritance of Coat Color Mutations

The inheritance of coat color mutations is a complex process that depends on the specific mutation involved. Some mutations are inherited in a dominant manner, while others are inherited in a recessive manner.

Dominant mutations: A dominant mutation is a mutation that is expressed in an individual who has only one copy of the mutated gene. For example, the white coat color mutation is a dominant mutation. This means that a dog with one copy of the white coat color gene will have a white coat.

Recessive mutations: A recessive mutation is a mutation that is only expressed in an individual who has two copies of the mutated gene. For example, the blue coat color mutation is a recessive mutation. This means that a dog must have two copies of the blue coat color gene in order to have a blue coat.

Understanding Coat Color Inheritance

Understanding the inheritance of coat color mutations is important for breeders who want to produce dogs with the desired coat colors. By understanding the genetics involved, breeders can make informed breeding decisions that will help them achieve their desired results.

Chapter 7: Fur Type Genetics

71 Different Fur Types in Rabbits

Rabbits, beloved for their soft and cuddly fur, exhibit a remarkable diversity in their coat characteristics. Each fur type serves a specific purpose and contributes to the rabbit's overall well-being and adaptability. Understanding these different types is crucial for proper rabbit care and appreciation of their unique features.

1. Normal Fur

Normal fur, the most common type, is characterized by its medium length, ranging from 1 to 3 inches. It consists of two layers: a dense undercoat that provides insulation and a longer guard hair layer that protects the undercoat from moisture and dirt. Normal fur requires regular brushing to prevent matting and promote overall coat health.

2. Rex Fur

Rex fur is distinguished by its short, plush, and velvety texture. It has a shorter guard hair layer and a dense, evenly textured undercoat. Rex fur's unique structure gives it a plush, soft feel and is highly sought after for its luxurious appearance. Regular brushing is necessary to maintain its soft and velvety texture.

3. Satin Fur

Satin fur is known for its glossy, silky appearance. It has a longer guard hair layer than normal fur, giving it a sheen and a distinctive shimmering effect. Satin fur is often used in show rabbits due to its eye-catching appearance. Regular brushing is recommended to prevent tangles and maintain its glossy shine.

4. Angora Fur

Angora fur is the longest and most luxurious of all rabbit fur types. It can grow up to 6 inches in length and is incredibly soft and fluffy. Angora fur is highly prized for its warmth and insulation properties. However, due to its length, it requires daily grooming to prevent matting and maintain its appearance.

5. Cashmere Fur

Cashmere fur, similar to Angora fur, is exceptionally soft and warm. It is typically shorter than Angora fur, ranging from 1 to 2 inches in length. Cashmere fur has a fine, dense texture that provides excellent insulation and is highly sought after for its luxurious feel. Regular brushing is necessary to prevent matting and maintain its softness.

6. Lilac Fur

Lilac fur is a unique and striking type of rabbit fur. It has a bluish-gray coloration and a soft, dense texture. Lilac fur is relatively easy to care for and requires regular brushing to maintain its appearance.

7. Ermine Fur

Ermine fur is characterized by its pure white coloration. It is a short, dense fur with a velvety texture. Ermine fur is highly prized for its pristine appearance and is often used in garments and accessories. Regular brushing is recommended to maintain its white color and soft texture.

Factors Influencing Fur Type

The type of fur a rabbit has is influenced by a combination of genetic and environmental factors. Genetics play a significant role in determining the length, texture, and color of the fur. Environmental factors, such as temperature and humidity, can also affect the coat's characteristics.

Conclusion

The diverse fur types in rabbits provide a fascinating insight into the adaptability and beauty of these fascinating creatures. Understanding these different types is essential for proper rabbit care, allowing us to appreciate and nurture the unique qualities of each rabbit companion.

72 Understanding the Genetics of Angora Fur

Angora fur, renowned for its exquisite softness and luxurious warmth, is a captivating natural fiber with a rich history and unique genetic characteristics. Its exceptional qualities have made it a highly sought-after material for centuries, prized by fashion designers and discerning consumers alike. To delve into the captivating world of Angora fur, it is essential to unravel the intricacies of its genetic makeup, which holds the key to understanding its remarkable properties.

The Angora Gene: A Tale of Mutations and Selective Breeding

The Angora gene, residing on a specific locus within the feline genome, is responsible for bestowing upon cats the distinctive trait of long, silky fur. This gene, denoted as L, exists in two primary alleles: L (dominant) and l (recessive). The dominant L allele, when present in homozygous form (LL), results in the expression of the Angora phenotype, characterized by an abundance of elongated, fine hair fibers. Conversely, cats with a homozygous recessive genotype (ll) possess short, dense fur. Heterozygous individuals (Ll), inheriting one dominant and one recessive allele, exhibit a semi-longhair phenotype, with fur length falling between that of Angoras and shorthair breeds.

The Angora gene's emergence is attributed to a spontaneous mutation that occurred within a domestic cat population. This mutation disrupted the normal function of a gene involved in hair follicle development, leading to the production of unusually long and silky hair fibers. Through selective breeding practices, humans have harnessed this genetic variation, preserving and propagating the Angora trait in specific feline lineages.

Beyond the Angora Gene: Modifier Genes and Polygenic Inheritance

While the Angora gene plays a pivotal role in determining fur length, it is not the sole genetic determinant. Modifier genes, acting in concert with the Angora gene, influence the overall quality and characteristics of the fur. These genes can affect fiber thickness, texture, and even color. The interplay between the Angora gene and modifier genes results in a wide range of phenotypic variations, contributing to the diversity observed within Angora cats.

Additionally, fur length in Angora cats exhibits polygenic inheritance, meaning that multiple genes contribute to the trait. The cumulative effect of these genes, each with its own small influence, shapes the final fur phenotype. This polygenic nature adds another layer of complexity to the genetics of Angora fur, underscoring the intricate interplay of genetic factors that determine this remarkable trait.

Environmental Factors and Phenotypic Expression

It is important to note that environmental factors can also impact the expression of the Angora gene. Nutrition, grooming practices, and overall health can influence the quality and appearance of the fur. Proper nutrition, rich in essential vitamins and minerals, supports healthy hair growth and maintenance. Regular grooming helps prevent tangles and mats, preserving the fur's softness and luster. Cats in good overall health tend to have healthier, more lustrous fur than those with underlying health conditions.

The Enchanting World of Angora Fur: A Tapestry of Genetics and Environment

The genetics of Angora fur are a testament to the remarkable diversity and complexity of the natural world. The Angora gene, modifier genes, and polygenic inheritance weave a intricate tapestry that gives rise to the exquisite beauty and luxurious warmth of Angora fur. By unraveling the genetic underpinnings of this captivating trait, we gain a deeper appreciation for the artistry of nature and the enduring legacy of human-animal partnerships.

73 The Rex Gene and its Influence on Fur Texture

Discovered in rabbits in the early 20th century, the rex gene has since been identified in a wide range of mammals, including cats, dogs, and even humans. This gene plays a crucial role in determining the softness, waviness, and overall appearance of fur, making it a subject of great interest to breeders and geneticists alike.

Molecular Basis of the Rex Gene

The rex gene encodes a protein known as keratin-associated protein 6-1 (KRTAP6-1). KRTAP6-1 is an essential component of the hair shaft, which is the primary structural element of fur. In individuals carrying the rex gene, a mutation occurs within the KRTAP6-1 gene, leading to the production of an altered protein. This altered protein disrupts the normal assembly and organization of the hair shaft, resulting in a unique and distinctive fur texture.

Phenotypic Effects of the Rex Gene

The most striking phenotypic effect of the rex gene is the alteration of fur texture. Fur in rex individuals is characterized by a soft, velvety feel due to the reduced number and size of guard hairs. Guard hairs are typically longer and coarser than underfur, providing protection and insulation. In rex animals, the reduction in guard hairs results in a more even and plush texture.

In addition to softness, the rex gene can also affect the waviness of fur. In some cases, rex animals exhibit a wavy or curly coat, while in others, the fur remains relatively straight. This variation in waviness is thought to be influenced by the specific type of mutation present in the rex gene.

Inheritance of the Rex Gene

The inheritance of the rex gene follows a simple Mendelian pattern. The rex allele is a dominant allele, meaning that individuals carrying only one copy of the rex gene (heterozygous) will exhibit the rex phenotype. Individuals who inherit two copies of the rex gene (homozygous) will have an even more pronounced rex phenotype.

Applications in Breeding and Genetics

The rex gene has significant implications for breeding and genetics. Breeders often seek out rex animals to create soft and luxurious fur in various breeds. In cats, for example, the rex gene gives rise to the distinctive curly-coated Cornish Rex breed. In dogs, the rex gene has been incorporated into breeds such as the Poodle and the Kerry Blue Terrier to enhance the softness and waviness of their coats.

Beyond breeding, the rex gene has also been used as a model to study genetic disorders affecting hair growth. Mutations in the KRTAP6-1 gene have been linked to conditions such as ectodermal dysplasia and brittle hair syndrome in humans. By understanding the molecular mechanisms underlying the rex gene, researchers can gain insights into the genetic basis of these disorders and develop potential treatments.

Conclusion

The rex gene is a captivating genetic variation that has a profound impact on the texture of animal fur. Its influence on softness, waviness, and overall appearance makes it a subject of great interest to breeders, geneticists, and animal enthusiasts alike. Understanding the molecular basis of the rex gene not only provides insights into the genetic control of fur development but also contributes to our knowledge of genetic disorders affecting hair growth. As research continues to unravel the complexities of the rex gene, its applications in breeding, genetics, and medicine are likely to expand even further in the future.

74 Rare Fur Type Mutations and their Characteristics

7. 4. 1 Introduction

Fur type mutations are relatively rare genetic variations that result in distinctive changes in the texture, length, or density of an animal's fur. These mutations can arise naturally through spontaneous genetic alterations or be artificially induced through selective breeding. Rare fur type mutations are often highly sought after by furriers and collectors due to their unique aesthetic appeal and perceived value.

7. 4. 2 Rex Mutations

One of the most well-known rare fur type mutations is the rex mutation. This mutation disrupts the normal growth pattern of the hair shaft, resulting in a plush, velvety texture. Rex mutations have been identified in various species, including rabbits, cats, and sheep.

7. 4. 2. 1 Rex Rabbits

The rex rabbit mutation was first discovered in 1919. Rex

rabbits are characterized by their short, dense fur that has a velvety feel. The fur is prized for its softness and insulating properties. Rex rabbits are commonly used for commercial fur production and as pets.

7. 4. 2. 2 Rex Cats

The rex cat mutation was first observed in 1950. Rex cats have a short, curly coat that gives them a distinctive appearance. The fur is soft and hypoallergenic, making it appealing to individuals with allergies. Rex cats are popular as companion animals.

7. 4. 2. 3 Rex Sheep

The rex sheep mutation was first reported in 1993. Rex sheep produce a highly sought-after wool that is characterized by its soft, curly texture. Rex wool is often blended with other fibers to create luxurious fabrics.

7. 4. 3 Angora Mutations

Angora mutations are another group of rare fur type mutations that result in the growth of long, flowing fur. Angora mutations have been identified in various species, including rabbits, cats, and goats.

7. 4. 3. 1 Angora Rabbits

The Angora rabbit mutation was first described in the 17th century. Angora rabbits have a dense, silky coat that can grow up to 12 inches in length. Angora wool is prized for its warmth, softness, and luxurious feel. Angora rabbits are raised primarily for their wool production.

7. 4. 3. 2 Angora Cats

The Angora cat mutation is believed to have originated in Turkey in the 16th century. Angora cats have a long, flowing coat that can come in various colors and patterns. The fur is soft and silky, giving Angora cats an elegant appearance. Angora cats are popular as companion animals.

7. 4. 3. 3 Angora Goats

The Angora goat mutation is believed to have originated in Turkey in the 15th century. Angora goats produce a lustrous, silky wool known as mohair. Mohair is highly prized for its warmth, softness, and durability. Angora goats are raised primarily for their mohair production.

7. 4. 4 Other Rare Fur Type Mutations

In addition to rex and angora mutations, numerous other rare fur type mutations have been identified. These mutations can result in a wide variety of fur characteristics, including:

Silky Mutations: Silky mutations disrupt the normal production of guard hairs, resulting in a silky, smooth coat.
Curly Mutations: Curly mutations alter the shape of the hair shaft, resulting in a curly or wavy coat.
Leopard Mutations: Leopard mutations create a distinctive spotted or leopard-like pattern on the fur.
Reverse Mutations: Reverse mutations result in the production of white or light-colored fur in animals that would normally have dark or pigmented fur.

7. 4. 5 Conclusion

Rare fur type mutations are genetic variations that result in distinctive changes in the texture, length, or density of an animal's fur. These mutations can be highly sought after for their unique aesthetic appeal and perceived value. Some of the most well-known rare fur type mutations include rex, angora, silky, curly, leopard, and reverse mutations. These mutations are found in various species, including rabbits, cats, sheep, and goats.

Chapter 8: Ear and Eye Color Genetics

81 The Genetics of Eye Color

The inheritance of eye color is a classic example of Mendelian genetics, and it has been instrumental in our understanding of how genes control the development of human traits. In this one, we will delve into the genetics of eye color, exploring the genes and alleles responsible for this diverse and captivating human characteristic.

The Basic Genetics of Eye Color

The color of our eyes is determined by the amount and distribution of melanin, a pigment that is produced by cells called melanocytes. Melanin is responsible for the pigmentation of our skin, hair, and eyes. There are two main types of melanin: eumelanin, which produces brown and black pigments, and pheomelanin, which produces red and yellow pigments.

The inheritance of eye color is controlled by a single gene called the OCA2 gene. The OCA2 gene is located on chromosome 15, and it contains two alleles: a dominant allele (B) that codes for brown eyes and a recessive allele (b) that codes for blue eyes.

Individuals who inherit two copies of the dominant allele

(BB) will have brown eyes. Individuals who inherit one copy of the dominant allele and one copy of the recessive allele (Bb) will also have brown eyes, because the dominant allele masks the effects of the recessive allele. However, individuals who inherit two copies of the recessive allele (bb) will have blue eyes, because there is no dominant allele to mask the effects of the recessive allele.

Other Factors that Influence Eye Color

While the OCA2 gene is the primary determinant of eye color, there are other genes and factors that can also influence the final color of our eyes. These include:

The amount of melanin in the iris: The more melanin in the iris, the darker the eyes will be.
The distribution of melanin in the iris: Melanin can be distributed evenly throughout the iris, or it can be concentrated in the center or around the edges of the iris. This can create different shades and patterns of eye color.
The presence of other pigments: In addition to melanin, there are other pigments that can be present in the iris, such as lipochrome and collagen. These pigments can contribute to the overall color of the eyes.
The thickness of the iris: The thicker the iris, the more light will be absorbed by the melanin, and the darker the eyes will be.
The age of the individual: Eye color can change slightly over time, as the amount and distribution of melanin in the iris changes.

Variations in Eye Color

The inheritance of eye color is not always straightforward. There are many different shades and variations of eye color, and some people even have eyes that are different colors. These variations are due to the complex interplay of the genes and factors that influence eye color.

Some of the most common eye colors include:

Brown: Brown eyes are the most common eye color in the world, and they are caused by a high concentration of melanin in the iris.
Blue: Blue eyes are caused by a low concentration of melanin in the iris. The blue color is due to the scattering of light by the collagen fibers in the iris.
Green: Green eyes are caused by a moderate concentration of melanin in the iris. The green color is due to the combination of blue and yellow pigments.
Hazel: Hazel eyes are a combination of brown and green. They are caused by a moderate concentration of melanin in the iris, and the color can vary depending on the lighting conditions.
Amber: Amber eyes are a rare eye color that is caused by a high concentration of lipochrome in the iris.

Conclusion

The genetics of eye color is a fascinating and complex field of study. While the OCA2 gene is the primary determinant of eye color, there are many other genes and factors that can also influence the final color of our eyes. The inheritance of eye color is not always straightforward, and there are many different shades and variations of eye color. These variations are due to the complex interplay of the genes and factors that influence eye color.

82 The Relationship Between Eye and Coat Color

The relationship between eye and coat color in dogs is a fascinating and complex one. While there are some general trends, there are also many exceptions to the rules. In general, dogs with light-colored coats tend to have lighter-colored eyes, while dogs with dark-colored coats tend to have darker-colored eyes. However, there are many dogs that do not fit this pattern. For example, some dogs with black coats have blue eyes, and some dogs with white coats have brown eyes.

The relationship between eye and coat color is determined by genetics. The genes that control coat color are different from the genes that control eye color. However, the two sets of genes can interact with each other to produce a variety of different coat and eye color combinations.

One of the most common ways that eye and coat color are linked is through the merle gene. The merle gene is a dominant gene that causes a mottled or speckled coat pattern. Dogs with the merle gene can have a variety of different coat colors, including blue, black, red, and sable. The merle gene can also affect eye color. Dogs with the merle gene often have blue or green eyes.

Another gene that can affect both eye and coat color is the piebald gene. The piebald gene is a recessive gene that causes white spotting on the coat. Dogs with the piebald gene can have a variety of different coat colors, including black, brown, and red. The piebald gene can also affect eye color. Dogs with the piebald gene often have blue or green eyes.

The relationship between eye and coat color is a complex one that is determined by genetics. There are many different genes that can affect both eye and coat color, and the interactions between these genes can produce a wide variety of different coat and eye color combinations.

8. 2. 1 Eye Color

The color of a dog's eyes is determined by the amount and type of melanin in the iris. Melanin is a pigment that is also responsible for the color of the skin and hair. Dogs with brown eyes have a high concentration of melanin in the iris, while dogs with blue eyes have a low concentration of melanin in the iris.

There are a variety of different factors that can affect the color of a dog's eyes, including:

Genetics: The genes that a dog inherits from its parents play a major role in determining the color of its eyes. Some genes are more likely to produce brown eyes, while other genes are more likely to produce blue eyes.
Age: The color of a dog's eyes can change over time. Puppies often have blue eyes that darken as they get older. This is because the amount of melanin in the iris increases as the dog ages.
Health: Certain health conditions can affect the color of a dog's eyes. For example, dogs with glaucoma often have green or yellow eyes.

8. 2. 2 Coat Color

The color of a dog's coat is determined by the type and amount of pigment in the hair. There are two main types of pigment in dog hair: eumelanin and pheomelanin.

Eumelanin is responsible for black and brown coat colors, while pheomelanin is responsible for red and yellow coat colors.

The amount and type of pigment in a dog's hair is determined by its genetics. Some genes are more likely to produce black hair, while other genes are more likely to produce red hair. The interaction between different genes can also produce a variety of different coat colors.

In addition to genetics, there are a number of other factors that can affect the color of a dog's coat, including:

Age: The color of a dog's coat can change over time. Puppies often have lighter-colored coats than adult dogs. This is because the amount of pigment in the hair increases as the dog ages.
Sun exposure: Sun exposure can lighten the color of a dog's coat. This is because the sun's ultraviolet rays can break down the pigment in the hair.
Diet: The diet of a dog can also affect the color of its coat. Dogs that eat a diet high in certain nutrients, such as zinc and copper, may have darker-colored coats.

83 The Genetics of Ear Size and Shape

The size and shape of the human ear are highly variable traits, with a wide range of normal variation. This variation is due to a combination of genetic and environmental factors.

Genetics of Ear Size

Ear size is primarily determined by genetics. Studies have

identified several genes that are involved in ear size regulation. These genes encode proteins that are involved in the development of the ear cartilage and other tissues.

One of the most important genes for ear size is called SOX9. This gene encodes a transcription factor that is essential for the development of cartilage. Mutations in the SOX9 gene can lead to a condition called campomelic dysplasia, which is characterized by short stature, bowed legs, and small ears.

Another gene that is involved in ear size is called FGF3. This gene encodes a growth factor that is involved in the development of the face and ears. Mutations in the FGF3 gene can lead to a condition called Crouzon syndrome, which is characterized by a small head, a flat face, and small ears.

Genetics of Ear Shape

The shape of the ear is also influenced by genetics. However, the genetic basis of ear shape is more complex than that of ear size. Several genes have been identified that are associated with ear shape, but each gene has only a small effect.

One of the genes that is associated with ear shape is called PAX6. This gene encodes a transcription factor that is involved in the development of the eye and ear. Mutations in the PAX6 gene can lead to a condition called aniridia, which is characterized by the absence of the iris. Aniridia is also associated with a distinctive ear shape, which is characterized by a small, pointed ear.

Another gene that is associated with ear shape is called PITX1. This gene encodes a transcription factor that is involved in the development of the pituitary gland and the inner ear. Mutations in the PITX1 gene can lead to a condition called Axenfeld-Rieger syndrome, which is characterized by glaucoma, iris abnormalities, and a distinctive ear shape.

Environmental Factors

In addition to genetics, environmental factors can also influence the size and shape of the ear. These factors include:

Prenatal exposure to alcohol or drugs: Prenatal exposure to alcohol or drugs can lead to a condition called fetal alcohol syndrome, which is characterized by a number of birth defects, including small ears.
Trauma: Trauma to the ear can lead to changes in the size and shape of the ear. This can occur as a result of an accident, surgery, or infection.
Aging: The size and shape of the ear can change with age. As people age, their ears tend to become larger and more floppy.

Conclusion

The size and shape of the human ear are highly variable traits, with a wide range of normal variation. This variation is due to a combination of genetic and environmental factors. Genetics plays a major role in determining ear size and shape, but environmental factors can also have an influence.

84 Understanding Genetic Predispositions for Ear Problems

Our ears are intricate organs that play a vital role in our ability to hear, balance, and process spatial information. While most people enjoy healthy hearing throughout their lives, some individuals are more susceptible to developing ear problems due to genetic factors. Understanding the genetic basis of ear disorders can help us identify those at risk, guide early intervention, and develop personalized treatment strategies.

Genetic Basis of Ear Problems

The genetic basis of ear problems can be attributed to mutations in various genes involved in the development and function of the ear. These mutations can be inherited from either parent or occur spontaneously as new mutations.

One of the most common genetic causes of ear problems is mutations in the GJB2 gene. GJB2 encodes a protein called connexin 26, which is essential for the formation of gap junctions in the inner ear. Gap junctions allow the passage of ions and molecules between cells, playing a crucial role in the transmission of electrical signals. Mutations in GJB2 can lead to hearing loss by disrupting the proper function of gap junctions in the inner ear.

Another gene associated with ear problems is SLC26A4. SLC26A4 encodes a protein involved in the transport of chloride ions across cell membranes. Mutations in SLC26A4 can result in a condition called Pendred syndrome, which is characterized by hearing loss, thyroid dysfunction, and balance problems.

Types of Ear Problems Linked to Genetics

The genetic mutations mentioned above can contribute to a

range of ear problems, including:

Hearing loss: Sensorineural hearing loss, the most common type of permanent hearing loss, can be caused by mutations in genes such as GJB2 and SLC26A4.
Tinnitus: Ringing or buzzing sounds in the ears can be a symptom of genetic disorders such as Pendred syndrome.
Balance problems: Vertigo and dizziness can be associated with genetic mutations that affect the vestibular system, the part of the inner ear responsible for balance.
Ear infections: Some genetic factors may increase susceptibility to chronic ear infections, such as otitis media.

Importance of Genetic Testing

Genetic testing can play a significant role in understanding the genetic basis of ear problems. By identifying specific mutations, genetic testing can:

Confirm a diagnosis of a genetic ear disorder.
Predict the risk of developing ear problems in individuals with a family history of these conditions.
Guide personalized treatment strategies based on the underlying genetic cause.

Conclusion

Genetic factors can contribute to the development of various ear problems. Understanding the genetic basis of these disorders allows us to identify those at risk, implement early intervention measures, and tailor treatment approaches to the specific genetic cause. Genetic testing can be a valuable tool in unraveling the genetic underpinnings of ear problems, empowering healthcare professionals and individuals alike to make informed decisions about their care and management.

Chapter 9: Body Type Genetics

91 The Influence of Genes on Body Size and Shape

Body size and shape are complex traits influenced by a combination of genetic and environmental factors. Genes play a significant role in determining an individual's height, weight, and body composition. While the environment, including factors such as nutrition, physical activity, and lifestyle, can also impact these traits, genetics sets the basic framework for our physical characteristics.

Height

Height is one of the most heritable human traits, with an estimated heritability of around 80%. This means that approximately 80% of the variation in height between individuals can be attributed to genetic differences. Genes involved in height regulation affect various aspects of skeletal growth, including the length of long bones and the size of growth plates.

Several specific genes have been identified as playing a role in height determination. For example, the FGFR3 gene encodes a protein involved in bone growth. Mutations in this gene can lead to conditions such as achondroplasia, a genetic disorder characterized by disproportionately short stature. Another gene, GH1, encodes growth hormone, a hormone essential for linear growth. Deficiencies in growth hormone can result in stunted growth.

Weight

Weight is another highly heritable trait, with an estimated heritability of around 40-60%. Genes involved in weight regulation affect various aspects of metabolism, appetite control, and energy expenditure.

The FTO gene has been extensively studied in relation to weight. This gene encodes a protein involved in appetite regulation. Variations in the FTO gene have been associated with increased body mass index (BMI) and obesity risk. Other genes implicated in weight regulation include the MC4R gene, which encodes a receptor for melanocortin hormones involved in appetite control, and the LEP gene, which encodes leptin, a hormone that signals satiety.

Body Composition

Body composition refers to the proportion of different tissues in the body, including muscle, fat, and bone. Genes also influence body composition, with an estimated heritability of around 50%.

The ACTN3 gene encodes a protein involved in muscle function. Variations in this gene have been associated with differences in muscle mass and athletic performance. Other genes implicated in body composition regulation include the PPARG gene, which encodes a receptor for peroxisome proliferator-activated receptor gamma, a transcription factor involved in adipogenesis (fat cell formation), and the UCP1 gene, which encodes uncoupling protein 1, a protein involved in thermogenesis (heat production).

Gene-Environment Interactions

While genes play a significant role in determining body size and shape, it is important to note that the environment also has a substantial impact. For example, nutrition can significantly influence growth and weight. Undernutrition during childhood can lead to stunted growth, while excessive calorie intake can contribute to obesity. Physical activity can also affect body composition, promoting muscle mass and reducing body fat.

Gene-environment interactions can also play a role in shaping body size and shape. For example, the effect of certain genetic variants on obesity risk may be influenced by dietary factors or physical activity levels.

Implications for Health and Disease

Understanding the genetic basis of body size and shape has implications for health and disease. For instance, individuals with genetic predispositions for obesity may benefit from early intervention and lifestyle modifications to reduce their risk of obesity-related diseases, such as heart disease, stroke, and type 2 diabetes. Conversely, individuals with genetic predispositions for tall stature may have an advantage in certain athletic endeavors, such as basketball or volleyball.

Conclusion

Genes play a significant role in determining body size and shape, influencing traits such as height, weight, and body composition. While the environment also has a substantial impact, genetics sets the basic framework for our physical characteristics. Understanding the genetic basis of these traits can provide insights into individual health risks and may help guide personalized interventions to promote optimal well-being.

92 Understanding the Genetics of Dwarfism

Dwarfism encompasses a heterogeneous group of genetic disorders characterized by short stature. While the average adult height is typically between 4'10" and 5'5" for individuals with dwarfism, there is considerable variation in height among different types. Dwarfism can result from mutations in genes that regulate growth hormone production, growth hormone signaling, or cartilage development.

Growth Hormone Deficiency

Growth hormone deficiency (GHD) is a condition in which the pituitary gland produces insufficient growth hormone, leading to impaired growth. GHD can be caused by genetic mutations that affect the production, secretion, or action of growth hormone. The most common genetic cause of GHD is mutations in the growth hormone-releasing hormone receptor (GHRHR) gene. Mutations in this gene disrupt the signaling pathway that triggers growth hormone release from the pituitary gland.

Growth Hormone Resistance

Growth hormone resistance occurs when the body does not respond to growth hormone signals properly. This can be caused by mutations in the growth hormone receptor (GHR) gene, which prevents the hormone from binding to its receptor on target cells. Mutations in other genes involved in the growth hormone signaling pathway can also lead to resistance.

Cartilage Development Disorders

Achondroplasia is the most common form of dwarfism, caused by mutations in the fibroblast growth factor receptor 3 (FGFR3) gene. FGFR3 plays a crucial role in cartilage development, and mutations in this gene result in the formation of abnormally short and thick bones. Other cartilage development disorders that can cause dwarfism include hypochondroplasia, pseudoachondroplasia, and multiple epiphyseal dysplasia.

Inheritance Patterns

The inheritance patterns of dwarfism vary depending on the specific genetic cause. GHD can be inherited in an autosomal dominant, autosomal recessive, or X-linked pattern. Achondroplasia is typically inherited in an autosomal dominant pattern, meaning that only one copy of the mutated FGFR3 gene is necessary to cause the condition. However, in some cases, achondroplasia can occur due to a spontaneous mutation.

Genetic Testing

Genetic testing can be used to identify mutations that cause dwarfism. This information can help in confirming the diagnosis, determining the inheritance pattern, and providing genetic counseling to affected individuals and their families. Genetic testing is recommended for individuals with dwarfism, especially if the cause is unknown or if there is a family history of the condition.

Conclusion

Dwarfism is a complex group of genetic disorders that result in short stature. The genetic basis of dwarfism can vary, including mutations in genes that regulate growth hormone production, growth hormone signaling, or cartilage development. Understanding the genetics of dwarfism is essential for accurate diagnosis, genetic counseling, and the development of potential therapeutic interventions. Advances in genetic research continue to shed light on the causes of dwarfism and improve the lives of individuals affected by these conditions.

93 Identifying Genetic Traits Associated with Body Type

Body type, often referred to as body composition, refers to the relative proportions of fat, muscle, and bone in an individual's body. It is a complex trait influenced by both genetic and environmental factors. Identifying the genetic traits associated with body type can provide valuable insights into understanding obesity, metabolic disorders, and other health conditions.

Genetic Determinants of Body Type

Numerous genetic variants have been identified as contributing to body type variation. These variants reside in genes involved in various biological pathways, including lipid metabolism, glucose homeostasis, and muscle development.

Adipogenesis and Lipid Metabolism

Adipogenesis, the process of fat cell formation, is a key

determinant of body fat mass. Genes involved in adipogenesis, such as PPARG and LPL, have been linked to body fat distribution. Variants in these genes can alter the rate and efficiency of adipogenesis, leading to variations in body fat percentage.

Glucose Homeostasis

Insulin resistance, a condition in which the body's cells become less responsive to insulin, is strongly associated with obesity. Genes involved in insulin signaling, such as IRS1 and PIK3R1, have been implicated in body type regulation. Variants in these genes can impair insulin sensitivity, leading to increased body fat accumulation.

Muscle Development

Muscle mass plays a significant role in body type. Genes involved in muscle development, such as ACTN3 and MSTN, have been associated with variations in muscle size and strength. Variants in these genes can affect muscle fiber composition, muscle growth potential, and overall body composition.

Environmental Factors and Gene-Environment Interactions

While genetics plays a substantial role in determining body type, environmental factors also have a significant impact. Diet, physical activity, and lifestyle choices can interact with genetic predispositions to influence body composition. For example, a high-fat diet can promote fat accumulation in individuals with certain genetic variants, while regular exercise can counteract the effects of obesity-promoting genes.

Clinical Implications and Future Directions

Understanding the genetic basis of body type has important clinical implications. It can help identify individuals at risk for obesity and related health conditions, such as type 2 diabetes and cardiovascular disease. Furthermore, it can guide personalized nutrition and exercise recommendations tailored to an individual's genetic profile.

Future research in this field aims to further elucidate the complex interplay between genetics, environment, and body type. Advances in genetic sequencing technologies and bioinformatics tools will enable the identification of additional genetic variants associated with body composition. Moreover, studies investigating gene-environment interactions will provide a more comprehensive understanding of the factors that shape body type.

94 Applying Genetic Knowledge for Selecting Healthy Rabbits

Genetics play a pivotal role in determining the health and well-being of rabbits. By understanding the genetic basis of inherited traits, rabbit breeders can make informed decisions to select animals that are less susceptible to disease and have a higher likelihood of expressing desirable health characteristics.

Genetic Predisposition to Diseases

Some rabbit breeds are more prone to developing certain diseases than others. For instance, dwarf breeds have a higher risk of developing joint and dental problems, while white rabbits are more susceptible to skin and eye issues. Breeders should be aware of these breed-specific health concerns and take steps to mitigate them through genetic selection.

Inbreeding and Linebreeding

Inbreeding, the mating of closely related individuals, can increase the likelihood of recessive genes being expressed. This can lead to the emergence of genetic disorders and reduced overall health. Conversely, linebreeding, the mating of individuals within a specific family line, can help maintain desirable traits and reduce the risk of introducing new genetic mutations. However, linebreeding must be practiced judiciously to avoid excessive inbreeding and the associated health risks.

DNA Testing and Genetic Markers

Advances in genetic technology have made it possible to identify specific genetic markers associated with particular diseases or health traits. DNA testing can be utilized to determine the presence of these markers and predict the likelihood of a rabbit developing a specific condition. This information can be invaluable for breeders seeking to select animals that are genetically predisposed to good health.

Selecting Rabbits for Breeding

When selecting rabbits for breeding, breeders should consider the following genetic factors:

Health history: Examine the health records of potential breeding stock and inquire about any known health conditions within their lineage.

Phenotype: Observe the physical characteristics of the rabbits, including their size, weight, fur quality, and overall appearance. Rabbits with a strong and healthy phenotype are more likely to pass on desirable genetic traits.
Genetic testing: If available, consider DNA testing for specific genetic markers associated with diseases or health traits. This information can provide valuable insights into the genetic makeup of the rabbits and guide breeding decisions.

Breeding Strategies for Health

Once healthy breeding stock has been selected, breeders can implement specific breeding strategies to promote genetic diversity and reduce the risk of inherited diseases. These strategies include:

Outcrossing: Introducing rabbits from unrelated lines into the breeding program to broaden the genetic pool.
Selective breeding: Mating individuals based on their desirable health characteristics and genetic makeup.
Hybridization: Crossing different breeds to create hybrids that inherit favorable traits from both parents.

Maintaining Genetic Records

Keeping accurate genetic records is essential for effective breeding programs. These records should include information on the ancestry, health history, and genetic test results of each rabbit. Well-maintained records allow breeders to track genetic lineages and make informed decisions about breeding strategies.

Ethical Considerations

While genetic knowledge can be a powerful tool for improving rabbit health, it is important to exercise ethical considerations when applying this knowledge. Breeders should prioritize the well-being of the animals and avoid practices that compromise their health or genetic integrity. Responsible genetic management practices ensure that future generations of rabbits inherit a legacy of good health and vitality.

Chapter 10: Genetic Health Considerations

101 Recognizing Common Genetic Health Issues in Rabbits

Rabbits are beloved companions, prized for their playful nature, soft fur, and endearing personalities. However, like all species, they can be prone to various health conditions, including those with a genetic basis. Understanding these genetic health issues is crucial for responsible rabbit ownership, enabling you to recognize symptoms, seek appropriate veterinary care, and make informed decisions about breeding practices.

10. 1. 1 Angora Wool Gene

The Angora wool gene (Aw) is a dominant trait responsible for the production of long, silky wool in Angora rabbits. While this wool is highly sought after for its luxurious texture, it comes with a significant health concern. Rabbits carrying the Aw gene often develop a life-threatening condition called "wool block. " As the rabbits' wool grows excessively, it can accumulate in their digestive tract, causing obstruction and ultimately leading to starvation. Regular shearing or plucking is essential to prevent wool block and maintain the health of Angora rabbits.

10. 1. 2 Dwarfism

Dwarfism in rabbits is caused by a recessive gene (dw). Rabbits homozygous for the dw gene (dw. dw) exhibit a shortened body and limbs, along with a round head and large eyes. While dwarf rabbits can be adorable, they are prone to several health complications. They may have difficulty breathing, experience dental problems, and face reduced mobility. Additionally, they are more susceptible to obesity and metabolic disorders.

10. 1. 3 Rex Gene

The Rex gene (Re) is responsible for the distinctive curly fur in Rex rabbits. This mutation affects the hair shaft's structure, resulting in a plush, velvety texture. While Rex rabbits are known for their unique appearance, they are predisposed to skin issues. Their curly fur can trap dirt and moisture, leading to skin irritation and the development of hot spots. Regular grooming and a clean environment are crucial for maintaining the health of Rex rabbits.

10. 1. 4 Satin Gene

The satin gene (Se) produces a glossy, lustrous coat in rabbits. This gene affects the hair shaft's refractive index, giving it a shimmering appearance. However, the satin gene also has an impact on the rabbit's overall health. Rabbits carrying the satin gene (Se. Se) are known to have weaker immune systems and are more susceptible to respiratory and digestive disorders. They may also have skin problems and decreased fertility.

10. 1. 5 Himalayan Gene

The Himalayan gene (C) is responsible for the distinctive

coloration pattern in Himalayan rabbits, characterized by a white body and dark points (ears, nose, tail). This gene affects the production of tyrosinase, an enzyme involved in melanin synthesis. Himalayan rabbits with the homozygous recessive genotype (cc) exhibit a completely white coat. While the Himalayan gene does not directly cause any health issues, it can be associated with an increased risk of cataract formation in older rabbits.

10. 1. 6 Conclusion

Understanding the common genetic health issues in rabbits is essential for their well-being and longevity. By recognizing the signs and symptoms associated with these conditions, rabbit owners can seek veterinary attention promptly and make informed decisions about breeding and care practices. Responsible rabbit ownership includes being aware of potential health risks, providing proper care, and ensuring the health and happiness of these beloved companions.

102 Understanding the Genetics of Hereditary Diseases

Hereditary diseases are disorders that are passed down from parents to children through genetic mutations. These mutations can disrupt the function of genes, leading to a wide range of symptoms and health problems. Understanding the genetics of hereditary diseases is essential for developing effective treatments and preventive measures.

Mendelian Inheritance

Gregor Mendel's laws of inheritance provide the foundation for understanding the transmission of hereditary diseases. Mendel's experiments with pea plants revealed that genes are passed down in discrete units, called alleles, and that each individual inherits two alleles for each gene, one from each parent.

In autosomal dominant inheritance, a single copy of the mutant allele is sufficient to cause the disease. Affected individuals inherit the mutant allele from one parent who is also affected (heterozygous) or from two parents who are carriers (homozygous). Examples of autosomal dominant disorders include Huntington's disease and Marfan syndrome.

In autosomal recessive inheritance, both copies of the gene must be mutated for the disease to manifest. Affected individuals inherit two copies of the mutant allele, one from each parent who is a carrier (heterozygous). Examples of autosomal recessive disorders include cystic fibrosis and sickle cell anemia.

X-linked Inheritance

X-linked inheritance refers to the transmission of genes located on the X chromosome. Males have only one X chromosome, while females have two. X-linked dominant disorders affect both males and females, but males are more severely affected because they have only one copy of the X chromosome. Examples of X-linked dominant disorders include Rett syndrome and Fragile X syndrome.

X-linked recessive disorders occur when a mutation in a gene on the X chromosome is inherited from the mother who is a carrier. Males with a single copy of the mutant allele are affected, while females with two copies of the mutant allele are carriers. Examples of X-linked recessive disorders include hemophilia and color blindness.

Mitochondrial Inheritance

Mitochondria are organelles within cells that produce energy. Mitochondrial DNA is inherited exclusively from the mother, so mitochondrial mutations are passed down only from mothers to children. Mitochondrial inheritance is associated with a range of disorders, including mitochondrial encephalomyopathy, lactic acidosis, and stroke-like episodes (MELAS) and Leigh syndrome.

Polygenic Inheritance

Some hereditary diseases are caused by the interaction of multiple genes, a phenomenon known as polygenic inheritance. These diseases often have a complex pattern of inheritance and can be influenced by environmental factors. Examples of polygenic disorders include diabetes, heart disease, and certain types of cancer.

Genetic Testing and Counseling

Genetic testing can identify mutations that cause hereditary diseases and provide information about an individual's risk of developing or passing on a disorder. Genetic counseling plays a vital role in interpreting genetic test results and providing support to individuals and families affected by hereditary diseases.

Conclusion

Understanding the genetics of hereditary diseases is crucial for developing effective treatments, providing genetic counseling, and implementing preventive measures. Mendelian inheritance patterns, X-linked inheritance, mitochondrial inheritance, and polygenic inheritance all contribute to the diversity of hereditary diseases. Genetic testing and counseling empower individuals and families to make informed decisions about their health and reproductive choices.

103 Identifying Genetic Markers for Disease Susceptibility

In the realm of medical research, the identification of genetic markers has emerged as a pivotal tool in unraveling the complex interplay between genes and disease susceptibility. Genetic markers, also known as genetic polymorphisms, are variations in the DNA sequence that can provide valuable insights into an individual's predisposition to certain diseases.

Genome-Wide Association Studies (GWAS)

One of the most significant advances in genetic marker identification has been the advent of genome-wide association studies (GWAS). GWAS involves scanning the entire human genome for variations that are associated with specific diseases. By comparing the genomes of individuals with and without a particular disease, researchers can pinpoint genetic variants that are more common in the affected group.

The strength of association between a genetic marker and a disease is typically measured by a statistical parameter called the odds ratio (OR). An OR greater than 1 indicates that individuals carrying a specific genetic variant are more likely to develop the disease, while an OR less than 1 suggests a protective effect.

Candidate Gene Approach

In addition to GWAS, researchers can also adopt a candidate gene approach to identify genetic markers. This approach focuses on genes that are known to be involved in specific biological pathways or functions that are implicated in a particular disease. By sequencing or genotyping these genes in individuals with and without the disease, researchers can identify specific variants that may contribute to disease susceptibility.

Exome Sequencing

Another powerful tool in genetic marker identification is exome sequencing. The exome represents the protein-coding portion of the genome, which is only about 1-2% of the total genome. However, it is estimated to contain over 85% of disease-associated genetic variants. Exome sequencing involves sequencing the entire exome of individuals with and without a disease, allowing researchers to identify rare variants that may contribute to disease susceptibility.

Next-Generation Sequencing (NGS)

The advent of next-generation sequencing (NGS) technologies has revolutionized the field of genetic marker identification. NGS platforms can sequence DNA or RNA much faster and more cost-effectively than traditional methods. This has enabled researchers to perform large-scale sequencing studies, including GWAS and exome sequencing, which would not have been feasible with previous technologies.

Applications of Genetic Markers

The identification of genetic markers for disease susceptibility has numerous applications in medicine and public health:

Disease Risk Assessment: Genetic markers can be used to predict an individual's risk of developing a particular disease based on their genetic profile. This information can help guide personalized preventive measures and early detection strategies.

Targeted Therapies: Genetic markers can be used to develop targeted therapies that are tailored to specific genetic subtypes of a disease. This approach can improve treatment efficacy and minimize side effects.

Pharmacogenomics: Genetic markers can help predict how individuals will respond to different medications, enabling personalized drug dosing and reducing adverse drug reactions.

Population Health: Genetic markers can be used to identify populations that are at high risk for certain diseases, allowing for targeted public health interventions and disease surveillance.

Challenges and Future Directions

While the identification of genetic markers has made significant progress, challenges remain in understanding the functional consequences of these variants and translating this knowledge into clinical practice. Future research will focus on:

Functional Studies: Determining the biological mechanisms

through which genetic markers contribute to disease susceptibility.

Polygenic Risk Scores: Combining multiple genetic markers to create polygenic risk scores that provide more accurate estimates of disease risk.

Gene-Environment Interactions: Understanding how genetic markers interact with environmental factors to influence disease risk.

Ethical and Social Implications: Addressing the ethical and social implications of genetic testing and ensuring equitable access to genetic information.

Conclusion

The identification of genetic markers for disease susceptibility has become an essential tool in medical research and personalized medicine. By leveraging advanced technologies and integrating genetic information into clinical practice, we can improve our understanding of disease etiology, develop more effective therapies, and ultimately enhance the health and well-being of individuals and populations.

104 Importance of Responsible Breeding Practices for Genetic Health

Responsible breeding practices are essential for maintaining the genetic health of any population, whether it be humans, animals, or plants. By carefully selecting breeding pairs and avoiding the mating of closely related individuals, breeders can reduce the risk of inherited disorders and maintain the genetic diversity of the population.

One of the most important reasons for responsible breeding

is to reduce the risk of inherited disorders. Many genetic disorders are caused by mutations in single genes, and these mutations can be passed on from parents to offspring. If two individuals who carry the same mutation mate, their offspring are at an increased risk of inheriting the disorder. Responsible breeders can reduce this risk by avoiding the mating of individuals who are known to carry harmful mutations.

Another important reason for responsible breeding is to maintain the genetic diversity of the population. Genetic diversity is essential for the long-term health of any population. It provides a buffer against environmental changes and allows the population to adapt to new challenges. When the genetic diversity of a population is reduced, the population becomes more vulnerable to disease and other threats.

Responsible breeding practices can help to maintain genetic diversity by ensuring that a wide range of genetic material is represented in the population. Breeders can do this by using a variety of breeding strategies, such as outcrossing and line breeding. Outcrossing involves the mating of individuals from different populations, while line breeding involves the mating of individuals who are closely related. Both of these strategies can help to increase the genetic diversity of the population.

In addition to reducing the risk of inherited disorders and maintaining genetic diversity, responsible breeding practices can also improve the overall health and well-being of the population. By selecting breeding pairs that are healthy and have good temperaments, breeders can produce offspring that are more likely to be healthy and well-behaved. Responsible breeding practices can also help to reduce the number of animals that are euthanized due to genetic disorders or behavioral problems. By carefully selecting breeding pairs and avoiding the mating of closely related individuals, breeders can reduce the risk of inherited disorders, maintain genetic diversity, and improve the overall health and well-being of the population.

Here are some specific examples of how responsible breeding practices can improve the genetic health of a population:

In humans, responsible breeding practices have helped to reduce the incidence of many inherited disorders, such as cystic fibrosis, sickle cell anemia, and Tay-Sachs disease. In animals, responsible breeding practices have helped to reduce the incidence of inherited disorders such as hip dysplasia in dogs, polycystic kidney disease in cats, and bloat in cattle.
In plants, responsible breeding practices have helped to develop new varieties that are resistant to pests and diseases, and that have improved yields and nutritional value.

Responsible breeding practices are an important part of any breeding program. By following these practices, breeders can help to ensure the genetic health of their animals and plants, and contribute to the overall health and well-being of the population.

Chapter 11: Breeding for Desired Traits

111 Setting Breeding Goals and Objectives

A breeding program is a long-term endeavor that requires careful planning and execution. The first step in developing a successful breeding program is to set clear goals and objectives. These goals and objectives will guide all aspects of the breeding program, from the selection of breeding stock to the evaluation of breeding results.

There are a number of factors to consider when setting breeding goals and objectives. These factors include:

The current status of the population. What are the strengths and weaknesses of the population. What are the major challenges facing the population.
The desired future state of the population. What are the goals for the population. What traits or characteristics are desired.
The resources available. What resources are available to support the breeding program. This includes financial resources, personnel, and facilities.

Once these factors have been considered, the breeder can begin to develop breeding goals and objectives. These goals and objectives should be specific, measurable, achievable, relevant, and time-bound (SMART).

Specific goals and objectives are clear and concise. They leave no room for interpretation. For example, a specific goal might be to increase the average daily gain of a population of cattle by 10%.

Measurable goals and objectives can be quantified. This allows the breeder to track progress towards the goal. For example, a measurable objective might be to reduce the incidence of a particular disease in a population of animals by 25%.

Achievable goals and objectives are realistic. They are not so ambitious that they are impossible to achieve. For example, an achievable goal might be to improve the reproductive efficiency of a population of swine by 5%.

Relevant goals and objectives are aligned with the overall goals of the breeding program. They are not simply "nice to have" goals. For example, a relevant goal might be to increase the profitability of a population of sheep.

Time-bound goals and objectives have a specific deadline. This creates a sense of urgency and helps to keep the breeding program on track. For example, a time-bound goal might be to achieve a particular breeding goal within five years.

Once breeding goals and objectives have been set, the breeder can begin to develop a breeding plan. The breeding plan will outline the specific steps that will be taken to achieve the breeding goals and objectives. The breeding plan should be reviewed and updated regularly to ensure that it is still on track.

Setting breeding goals and objectives is an essential step in developing a successful breeding program. By taking the time to carefully consider all of the factors involved, the breeder can set goals and objectives that will help to achieve the desired future state of the population.

Additional Considerations

In addition to the factors discussed above, there are a number of other considerations that may be relevant when setting breeding goals and objectives. These considerations include:

The genetic diversity of the population. The genetic diversity of a population is a measure of the amount of genetic variation within the population. A population with a high level of genetic diversity is more likely to be able to adapt to changing environmental conditions.

The genetic relationships among individuals in the population. The genetic relationships among individuals in a population can affect the rate of genetic progress. In general, the closer the genetic relationship between two individuals, the more similar they will be in terms of their genetic makeup.

The heritability of the traits being selected for. The heritability of a trait is a measure of the extent to which the trait is passed from parents to offspring. Traits with a high heritability are more likely to respond to selection than traits with a low heritability.

The economic value of the traits being selected for. The economic value of a trait is a measure of the impact that the trait has on the profitability of the enterprise. Traits with a high economic value are more likely to be selected for than traits with a low economic value.

By considering all of these factors, the breeder can set breeding goals and objectives that will help to achieve the desired future state of the population.

112 Selecting Breeding Pairs Based on Genetics

By selecting breeding pairs based on their genetic characteristics, breeders can harness the power of inheritance to produce offspring with desired traits, enhance productivity, and maintain genetic diversity within their herds or flocks.

Principles of Genetic Selection

Genetic selection relies on the principles of inheritance, which dictate the transmission of genetic material from parents to offspring. Each individual inherits half of its genetic material from its mother and half from its father. This genetic material, in the form of chromosomes and genes, carries the instructions for various traits, including physical characteristics, performance attributes, and disease resistance.

Breeders can utilize genetic information to identify individuals with superior genetic potential for specific traits. These individuals are then selected as breeding pairs, increasing the likelihood that their offspring will inherit these desirable traits. The process of genetic selection is iterative, with each generation providing an opportunity to further refine and improve the genetic makeup of the herd or flock.

Methods of Genetic Selection

Several methods of genetic selection are commonly employed, including:

Phenotypic selection: Selecting individuals based on their observable traits or performance records. This method is straightforward and widely used but relies on accurate phenotyping and can be influenced by environmental factors.

Genomic selection: Utilizing genetic information from high-throughput genotyping technologies to predict the genetic merit of individuals. Genomic selection allows for early and precise selection, even before individuals have expressed their phenotypes.

Pedigree selection: Using the known genetic relationships among individuals to estimate their genetic potential. Pedigree selection relies on accurate pedigree records and can be less precise than genomic selection.

Consideration of Genetic Diversity

While selecting breeding pairs based on genetics is essential for improving traits, breeders must also consider maintaining genetic diversity within their herds or flocks. Genetic diversity ensures resilience, adaptability, and reduces the risk of inbreeding depression, a condition that arises from the mating of closely related individuals.

Breeders can maintain genetic diversity by introducing unrelated individuals into their breeding programs, avoiding excessive inbreeding, and utilizing crossbreeding strategies. By balancing genetic selection with the preservation of genetic diversity, breeders can create healthy, productive, and sustainable livestock populations.

Ethical Considerations

Genetic selection raises ethical considerations related to the manipulation of animal genetics. Breeders must ensure that their selection practices do not compromise the welfare or health of their animals. They must also consider the potential long-term consequences of genetic changes on the genetic integrity and biodiversity of the species.

Conclusion

Selecting breeding pairs based on genetics is a powerful tool for animal breeders. By harnessing the principles of inheritance and employing various genetic selection methods, breeders can improve the genetic makeup of their livestock, achieve specific breeding goals, and maintain genetic diversity. However, ethical considerations must be carefully weighed to ensure the well-being of animals and the preservation of genetic heritage.

113 Utilizing Line Breeding and Inbreeding Strategies

Line breeding involves mating individuals within a closely related group, such as siblings or half-siblings, while inbreeding refers to the mating of parents and offspring or full siblings. Both techniques aim to increase the frequency of desirable traits and reduce genetic variation within a population.

Line Breeding

Line breeding is a less extreme form of inbreeding that involves mating individuals within a defined breeding line. This line is typically established by selecting a superior individual and breeding it to its offspring or close relatives. The resulting offspring are then interbred to further concentrate the desired traits. Line breeding can be used to improve specific characteristics, such as growth rate, disease resistance, or conformation.

Advantages of Line Breeding:

Increased homozygosity: Line breeding increases the frequency of homozygous genotypes, which results in more uniform and predictable offspring.
Concentration of desirable traits: By mating individuals with similar genetic backgrounds, line breeding allows breeders to concentrate specific traits within the line.
Reduced inbreeding depression: Line breeding can reduce the negative effects of inbreeding depression, such as reduced fertility and increased susceptibility to disease, by avoiding extreme matings.

Disadvantages of Line Breeding:

Limited genetic diversity: Line breeding can reduce genetic diversity within a population, which can make it more susceptible to environmental stressors and disease outbreaks.
Increased risk of genetic defects: The concentration of homozygous genotypes can increase the risk of exposing recessive genetic defects that may otherwise be hidden in heterozygous individuals.
Slow genetic progress: Line breeding can be a slow process, as it requires several generations of selective breeding to achieve desired results.

Inbreeding

Inbreeding involves the mating of parents and offspring or full siblings. This extreme form of line breeding results in a higher degree of genetic uniformity and homozygosity compared to line breeding. Inbreeding is often used in research settings to study the effects of genetic variation on specific traits.

Advantages of Inbreeding:

Rapid genetic progress: Inbreeding can accelerate genetic progress by quickly concentrating desired traits within a population.
Increased genetic uniformity: Inbreeding produces offspring with a high degree of genetic uniformity, making it easier to predict their performance.
Identification of genetic defects: Inbreeding can help identify recessive genetic defects that may be hidden in heterozygous individuals.

Disadvantages of Inbreeding:

Severe inbreeding depression: Inbreeding can lead to severe inbreeding depression, including reduced fertility, increased susceptibility to disease, and decreased vigor.
Loss of genetic diversity: Inbreeding significantly reduces genetic diversity, making populations more vulnerable to environmental changes and disease outbreaks.
Ethical concerns: Inbreeding can raise ethical concerns, particularly when it involves the mating of close relatives, such as siblings.

Considerations for Utilizing Line Breeding and Inbreeding

When utilizing line breeding or inbreeding strategies, it is crucial to consider the following factors:

Breeding goals: Clearly define the specific traits that you want to improve through line breeding or inbreeding.
Genetic diversity: Monitor genetic diversity within the breeding population to avoid excessive inbreeding depression.
Inbreeding coefficient: Use inbreeding coefficients to track the level of inbreeding and manage the risk of genetic defects.
Outcrossing: Incorporate outcrossing into the breeding program periodically to introduce new genetic material and reduce inbreeding depression.
Ethical implications: Consider the ethical implications of inbreeding, especially when it involves the mating of close relatives.

Conclusion

Line breeding and inbreeding are powerful strategies that can be used to improve genetic uniformity and predictability in breeding programs. However, it is important to carefully consider the potential benefits and risks associated with each technique. By understanding the advantages and disadvantages of line breeding and inbreeding, breeders can make informed decisions about when and how to utilize these strategies to achieve their breeding goals.

114 Avoiding Inbreeding Depression and Genetic Problems

Inbreeding depression is a phenomenon that occurs when individuals within a population mate with each other over several generations. This can lead to an increase in the frequency of homozygous genotypes, which can be detrimental to the health and fitness of the population. Inbreeding depression can occur in any species, including humans, animals, and plants.

There are a number of factors that can contribute to inbreeding depression, including:

Genetic drift: This is the random change in the frequency of alleles in a population. Genetic drift can lead to the loss of genetic diversity, which can make a population more susceptible to inbreeding depression.
Mutation: Mutations are changes in the DNA sequence. Mutations can be harmful, beneficial, or neutral. Harmful mutations can contribute to inbreeding depression by reducing the fitness of individuals.
Selection: Selection is the process by which certain traits are favored over others. Selection can lead to the increase in the frequency of beneficial alleles in a population. However, selection can also lead to the increase in the frequency of harmful alleles in a population, which can contribute to inbreeding depression.

Inbreeding depression can have a number of negative consequences for a population, including:

Reduced fitness: Inbred individuals are often less fit than outbred individuals. This can be due to a number of factors, including reduced fertility, increased susceptibility to disease, and decreased growth rate.
Increased homozygosity: Inbred individuals have a higher frequency of homozygous genotypes than outbred

individuals. This can lead to the expression of harmful recessive alleles that would otherwise be masked by dominant alleles.

Increased genetic load: The genetic load is the total number of harmful alleles in a population. Inbreeding can increase the genetic load of a population by increasing the frequency of harmful recessive alleles.

There are a number of ways to avoid inbreeding depression, including:

Outbreeding: Outbreeding is the mating of individuals from different populations. Outbreeding can increase genetic diversity and reduce the frequency of harmful recessive alleles.

Selective breeding: Selective breeding is the mating of individuals with desired traits. Selective breeding can be used to improve the fitness of a population and reduce the frequency of harmful alleles.

Genetic counseling: Genetic counseling can help individuals understand the risks of inbreeding and make informed decisions about mating.

Inbreeding depression is a serious problem that can have a number of negative consequences for a population. However, there are a number of ways to avoid inbreeding depression, including outbreeding, selective breeding, and genetic counseling.

Additional Information

In addition to the information provided above, there are a few other things that you can do to avoid inbreeding depression in your breeding program. These include:

Keep accurate records: It is important to keep accurate records of the pedigrees of your animals. This will help you to identify and avoid mating closely related individuals. Use a variety of breeding stock: When selecting breeding stock, it is important to use a variety of individuals from different genetic backgrounds. This will help to increase genetic diversity and reduce the risk of inbreeding depression.

Avoid breeding from animals with known genetic defects: If you know that an animal has a genetic defect, it is important to avoid breeding from that animal. This will help to prevent the spread of the defect to other animals in your population.

By following these tips, you can help to avoid inbreeding depression and maintain the health and fitness of your breeding program.

Chapter 12: Pedigree Analysis

121 Understanding the Importance of Pedigrees

12. 1. 1 Introduction to Pedigrees

A pedigree is a diagram that represents the inheritance of traits within a family or group of individuals. It is a valuable tool for understanding the genetic relationships between family members and for tracing the inheritance of specific traits, both desirable and undesirable. Pedigrees can help researchers identify patterns of inheritance, predict the likelihood of an individual inheriting a particular trait, and provide insights into the genetic basis of complex diseases.

12. 1. 2 Types of Pedigrees

Pedigrees can be classified into two main types:

1. Vertical Pedigree: This type of pedigree represents the inheritance of traits over multiple generations. Individuals are arranged in vertical columns, with each generation represented by a separate row. Vertical pedigrees are particularly useful for tracing the inheritance of rare or dominant traits.

2. Horizontal Pedigree: This type of pedigree represents the inheritance of traits within a single generation. Individuals are arranged in horizontal rows, with each individual

representing a sibling. Horizontal pedigrees are particularly useful for studying the inheritance of recessive traits.

12. 1. 3 Symbols Used in Pedigrees

To represent individuals and their genetic relationships, pedigrees use a standardized set of symbols:

Square: Represents a male individual.
Circle: Represents a female individual.
Filled Square. Circle: Represents an individual affected with the trait of interest.
Open Square. Circle: Represents an individual not affected with the trait of interest.
Diagonal Line: Represents a deceased individual.
Vertical Line: Represents a mating between two individuals.
Horizontal Line: Represents offspring from a mating.

12. 1. 4 Importance of Pedigrees

Pedigrees play a crucial role in genetic research and counseling due to their ability to:

1. Identify Patterns of Inheritance: Pedigrees can help identify the inheritance pattern of a trait, such as whether it is dominant, recessive, X-linked, or autosomal. This information is essential for understanding how a trait is passed on from generation to generation.

2. Predict Trait Inheritance: Based on the inheritance pattern, pedigrees can provide an estimate of the probability that an individual will inherit or pass on a particular trait. This information can be valuable for individuals planning to have children or for those who are at risk for inheriting a genetic disease.

3. Identify Carriers of Genetic Diseases: Pedigrees can help identify individuals who carry a genetic mutation even if they do not exhibit the associated disease. Carriers have one copy of the mutation and can pass it on to their children, increasing the risk of the child developing the disease.

4. Study Complex Diseases: Pedigrees are essential tools for studying the inheritance of complex diseases, such as heart disease, cancer, and diabetes. By examining the inheritance patterns in multiple families, researchers can identify genetic factors that contribute to these diseases and develop strategies for prevention and treatment.

5. Provide Genetic Counseling: Pedigrees are used in genetic counseling to help individuals understand their genetic risks and make informed decisions about their reproductive choices. Counselors can use pedigrees to assess the likelihood of inheriting or passing on a particular trait and provide guidance on options for testing and family planning.

12. 1. 5 Conclusion

Pedigrees are invaluable tools for understanding the inheritance of traits within families. They provide a visual representation of genetic relationships and patterns of inheritance, allowing researchers and genetic counselors to identify carriers of genetic diseases, predict the probability of inheriting specific traits, and study the genetic basis of complex diseases. By understanding the importance of pedigrees, individuals can gain valuable insights into their own genetic inheritance and make informed choices about their reproductive health.

122 Reading and Interpreting Pedigree Charts

Pedigree charts, also known as family trees, are invaluable tools for visualizing and analyzing the inheritance patterns of traits within a family. They provide a graphical representation of the relationships between individuals and the phenotypic expression of specific traits, allowing researchers and healthcare professionals to infer the mode of inheritance and identify genetic risks.

12. 2 Reading and Interpreting Pedigree Charts

Components of a Pedigree Chart:

Symbols: Individuals are represented by standard symbols, with squares for males and circles for females.
Generations: Individuals are arranged in horizontal rows, with each row representing a generation.
Connections: Lines connect individuals to indicate their relationships (e. g. , parents, siblings).
Shading: Shaded symbols indicate individuals who express a particular trait or phenotype.

Reading a Pedigree Chart:

1. Identify the Proband: The individual with the trait of interest is known as the proband and is usually marked with an arrow.
2. Trace Relationships: Follow the lines to determine the relationships between individuals. Solid lines indicate biological relationships, while dashed lines indicate adopted or half-sibling relationships.
3. Observe Phenotypes: Note the shaded symbols to identify individuals who express the trait of interest.

4. Infer Inheritance: By examining the distribution of phenotypes among family members, you can infer the mode of inheritance (e. g. , dominant, recessive, X-linked).

Interpreting Inheritance Patterns:

Dominant Inheritance:

A single copy of the dominant allele (A) is sufficient to express the trait.
Affected individuals have at least one shaded parent.
Unaffected individuals have two unshaded parents.

Recessive Inheritance:

Two copies of the recessive allele (a) are required to express the trait.
Affected individuals have two shaded parents.
Carriers (heterozygotes) have one shaded and one unshaded parent and do not express the trait.

X-Linked Inheritance:

The gene responsible for the trait is located on the X chromosome.
Males are typically hemizyguous for X-linked genes (one copy), while females are heterozygous (two copies).
Males with X-linked recessive disorders are affected, while females are typically carriers.

Other Features:

Consanguinity: Individuals with common ancestors are said to be consanguineous. Consanguinity increases the likelihood of recessive disorders.

Sporadic Cases: Some traits may appear in a family without a clear inheritance pattern, suggesting a spontaneous mutation or environmental factors.

Adoption: Adopted individuals may not have genetic relationships to their listed parents.

Unknown Genotypes: In some cases, the genotypes of individuals may be unknown, which can limit the interpretation of the pedigree.

Importance of Pedigree Charts:

Pedigree charts serve numerous important functions:

Diagnosis: By identifying inheritance patterns, pedigree charts can aid in diagnosing genetic disorders.

Predictive Risk Assessment: They can estimate the probability of an individual inheriting or passing on a particular trait.

Genetic Counseling: Pedigree charts help genetic counselors provide information and support to families at risk for genetic conditions.

Population Genetics: Analysis of pedigree charts can provide insights into the frequency and distribution of genetic traits within populations. By understanding the components and inheritance patterns represented in these charts, researchers and healthcare professionals can gain valuable insights into the genetic basis of traits, diagnose genetic disorders, and provide genetic counseling.

123 Identifying Genetic Traits Through Pedigree Analysis

Pedigree analysis is a valuable tool for geneticists and medical professionals to study the inheritance patterns of genetic traits within families. It involves constructing a diagrammatic representation of a family tree, tracing the transmission of specific traits across generations. By analyzing pedigrees, researchers can identify the mode of inheritance, estimate the risk of inheriting a particular trait, and provide genetic counseling to individuals and families.

Basic Principles of Pedigree Analysis

Pedigree charts use standard symbols to represent individuals and their relationships. Squares represent males, circles represent females, and horizontal lines connect spouses. Vertical lines descend from each individual to represent their offspring. Affected individuals are typically shaded or filled in, while unaffected individuals are left open.

The mode of inheritance can be inferred from the pattern of trait transmission in a pedigree. Autosomal dominant traits are expressed in individuals who inherit at least one copy of the dominant allele from either parent. In a pedigree, affected individuals will have at least one affected parent, and the trait will appear in every generation. Autosomal recessive traits, on the other hand, are only expressed in individuals who inherit two copies of the recessive allele, one from each parent. In a pedigree, affected individuals typically have two unaffected parents, and the trait may skip generations.

Identifying Inheritance Patterns

Pedigree analysis can help identify the inheritance pattern of genetic traits. Some common inheritance patterns include:

Autosomal dominant: Trait is expressed in individuals with

at least one dominant allele.

Autosomal recessive: Trait is expressed only in individuals with two copies of the recessive allele.

X-linked dominant: Trait is expressed in females with one copy of the dominant allele and in males with one copy of the dominant allele on the X chromosome.

X-linked recessive: Trait is expressed in males with one copy of the recessive allele on the X chromosome and in females with two copies of the recessive allele.

Calculating Inheritance Risk

Pedigree analysis can also be used to estimate the risk of inheriting a particular trait. For example, if an individual has an affected parent who is heterozygous for an autosomal dominant trait, the individual has a 50% chance of inheriting the trait. If an individual has two unaffected parents, but both are carriers for an autosomal recessive trait, the individual has a 25% chance of being affected.

Genetic Counseling

Pedigree analysis is a crucial tool in genetic counseling, which involves providing information and support to individuals and families at risk for inherited disorders. Genetic counselors use pedigrees to assess family history, identify inheritance patterns, and estimate the risk of developing or transmitting genetic conditions. They can also provide guidance on reproductive options, screening tests, and preventive measures.

Limitations of Pedigree Analysis

While pedigree analysis is a powerful tool, it has certain limitations:

Incomplete information: Pedigrees may not always include all relevant information, such as miscarriages, adoptions, or unknown paternity.

Variable expressivity: Some genetic traits exhibit variable expressivity, meaning that individuals with the same genotype may have different degrees of the trait's manifestation.

Genetic heterogeneity: Some genetic traits may be caused by mutations in different genes, leading to similar phenotypes but different inheritance patterns.

Despite these limitations, pedigree analysis remains an essential tool for understanding genetic inheritance and providing valuable information for genetic counseling.

124 Using Pedigrees for Future Breeding Decisions

They provide a visual representation of an individual's genetic heritage, allowing breeders to track the inheritance of desirable and undesirable traits. By understanding the genetic relationships within a population, breeders can select individuals with complementary traits to produce offspring with enhanced performance and reduced risk of inherited disorders.

Pedigree Analysis

The first step in using pedigrees for breeding decisions is to construct a comprehensive pedigree that includes multiple generations. This can be done using software or manual record-keeping. The pedigree should include information on each individual's parents, grandparents, and siblings, as well as their performance data (e. g. , growth rate, disease resistance, reproductive success).

Once the pedigree is constructed, breeders can analyze it to identify genetic patterns and relationships. This involves examining the frequency of certain traits, the inheritance of dominant and recessive alleles, and the occurrence of genetic disorders. Breeders can also use statistical methods to calculate inbreeding coefficients, which measure the degree of genetic relatedness within a population.

Selective Breeding

Based on the pedigree analysis, breeders can make informed decisions about which individuals to select for breeding. Selective breeding involves choosing individuals with desirable traits and mating them to produce offspring that inherit these traits. Breeders can use pedigrees to identify individuals with a high genetic potential for specific traits, such as fast growth, high milk production, or disease resistance.

When selecting individuals for breeding, breeders should consider the following factors:

Phenotype: The observable traits of an individual, which are influenced by both genotype and environment.
Genotype: The genetic makeup of an individual, which determines their potential to express certain traits.
Heritability: The proportion of phenotypic variation that is due to genetic factors.

Outcrossing and Inbreeding

In addition to selective breeding, breeders may also use

outcrossing or inbreeding to manage genetic diversity within a population. Outcrossing involves mating individuals from different populations to introduce new genetic material, which can increase genetic diversity and reduce the risk of inherited disorders. Inbreeding, on the other hand, involves mating individuals from the same population to concentrate desirable traits or reduce the expression of undesirable traits. However, inbreeding can also increase the risk of genetic disorders due to the increased homozygosity for recessive alleles.

Ethical Considerations

While pedigrees can be a powerful tool for breeding decisions, it is important for breeders to use them ethically. Breeders should avoid excessive inbreeding, which can lead to genetic disorders and health problems. They should also consider the welfare of the animals they are breeding, ensuring that they are not subject to inhumane treatment or excessive genetic manipulation.

Conclusion

Pedigrees are an essential tool for breeders to make informed decisions about future breeding programs. By understanding the genetic relationships within a population, breeders can select individuals with complementary traits to produce offspring with enhanced performance and reduced risk of inherited disorders. Pedigrees also allow breeders to manage genetic diversity through outcrossing and inbreeding, while ensuring the ethical treatment of animals.

Chapter 13: Genetic Testing in Rabbits

131 The Availability of Genetic Tests for Rabbits

The field of veterinary genetics has made significant advancements in recent years, leading to the development of various genetic tests for rabbits. These tests play a crucial role in diagnosing inherited diseases, determining breed predispositions, and guiding breeding programs to improve the overall health and well-being of rabbits.

Types of Genetic Tests for Rabbits

Genetic tests for rabbits can be categorized based on their purpose and the type of genetic information they analyze. Some of the most common types include:

Single-gene tests: These tests focus on detecting mutations in a specific gene known to cause a particular inherited disease. Examples include tests for dwarfism, angora wool, and certain types of eye disorders.

Multi-gene panels: These tests simultaneously screen for mutations in multiple genes associated with a range of inherited conditions. They provide a comprehensive assessment of a rabbit's genetic health and can be particularly useful in identifying carriers of recessive diseases.

Breed-specific tests: These tests are designed to detect genetic markers that are characteristic of specific rabbit breeds. They can be used to verify breed purity, identify breed-related health issues, and assist in breed conservation efforts.

DNA profiling: DNA profiling involves analyzing the unique genetic fingerprint of an individual rabbit. This information can be used for parentage verification, identification of lost or stolen animals, and forensic investigations.

Availability of Genetic Tests

The availability of genetic tests for rabbits has increased substantially in recent years. Several commercial laboratories and veterinary clinics now offer a wide range of tests, catering to the needs of rabbit owners, breeders, and veterinarians. The specific tests available may vary depending on the laboratory or clinic, but most offer a comprehensive suite of options.

Factors Influencing Test Availability

The availability of genetic tests for rabbits can be influenced by several factors, including:

Disease prevalence: Tests for diseases that are more common in rabbits are typically more readily available.

Technological advancements: As genetic sequencing technologies continue to evolve, new tests are being developed and existing tests become more affordable and accessible.

Market demand: Laboratories and clinics respond to the demand for specific tests, ensuring that the most sought-after tests are widely available.

Veterinary expertise: Veterinarians play a key role in educating rabbit owners about genetic testing options and facilitating access to these tests.

Accessing Genetic Tests

Rabbit owners who are interested in pursuing genetic testing for their animals should consult with a veterinarian. Veterinarians can provide guidance on the most appropriate tests based on the rabbit's breed, health history, and the owner's concerns. They can also assist with sample collection and interpretation of test results.

Importance of Genetic Testing

Genetic testing offers numerous benefits for rabbits, including:

Early diagnosis and treatment: Genetic tests can help diagnose inherited diseases at an early stage, allowing for prompt treatment and management.

Prevention of disease transmission: Identifying carriers of genetic diseases can prevent the spread of these conditions within breeding programs and the general rabbit population.

Improved breeding practices: Genetic testing provides valuable information for selective breeding, enabling breeders to produce healthier and more resilient rabbits.

Conservation of genetic diversity: Breed-specific tests can help maintain the genetic integrity of rare or endangered rabbit breeds.

Conclusion

Genetic testing has become an essential tool in the field of rabbit health and breeding. The availability of a wide range of tests allows rabbit owners and veterinarians to make informed decisions regarding the health and well-being of their animals. By harnessing the power of genetic information, we can improve the lives of rabbits and contribute to the preservation of their genetic heritage.

132 Understanding the Purpose of Genetic Testing

Genetic testing is a powerful tool that can provide valuable information about a person's health and risk of developing certain diseases. It can be used to diagnose genetic conditions, predict the likelihood of developing a disease, and determine the best course of treatment. However, it is important to understand the purpose of genetic testing and the potential implications before making a decision about whether or not to undergo testing.

There are many different types of genetic tests, each with its own specific purpose. Some tests are used to diagnose genetic conditions, such as cystic fibrosis or Huntington's disease. These tests can provide a definitive diagnosis, which can help guide treatment and management decisions. Other tests are used to predict the likelihood of developing a disease, such as breast cancer or Alzheimer's disease. These tests can help people make informed decisions about their health and lifestyle choices. Still other tests are used to determine the best course of treatment for a particular disease. For example, genetic testing can be used to identify the most effective medication for a particular type of cancer.

Genetic testing can have a significant impact on a person's life. A positive test result can lead to a diagnosis of a serious illness, which can be emotionally devastating. It can also lead to discrimination or insurance problems. A negative test result can be a relief, but it does not guarantee that a person will never develop a disease. It is important to weigh the potential benefits and risks of genetic testing before making a decision about whether or not to undergo testing.

There are a number of factors to consider when making a decision about genetic testing. These include:

The type of test being considered
The reason for testing
The potential benefits and risks of testing
The emotional and financial costs of testing
The availability of support and resources

It is important to discuss these factors with a healthcare professional before making a decision about genetic testing. A healthcare professional can help explain the benefits and risks of testing and can help you decide if testing is right for you.

Here are some additional points to consider when making a decision about genetic testing:

Genetic testing is not a perfect science. There is always a

chance of a false positive or false negative result.

Genetic testing can be expensive. The cost of testing can vary depending on the type of test and the laboratory that performs the test.

Genetic testing can have a significant impact on a person's life. It is important to be prepared for the potential emotional and financial consequences of testing.

There are a number of support and resources available to people who are considering genetic testing. These resources can help people understand the benefits and risks of testing and can provide emotional support.

Genetic testing is a powerful tool that can provide valuable information about a person's health. However, it is important to understand the purpose of genetic testing and the potential implications before making a decision about whether or not to undergo testing. By weighing the potential benefits and risks and by considering the factors discussed above, you can make an informed decision about whether or not genetic testing is right for you.

133 Interpreting Genetic Test Results

The interpretation of genetic test results is a complex process that requires careful consideration of a variety of factors, including the type of test, the individual's personal and family history, and the potential implications of the results.

Types of Genetic Tests

There are two main types of genetic tests: diagnostic tests and screening tests. Diagnostic tests are used to confirm or rule out a specific genetic condition, while screening tests are used to identify individuals who may be at risk for developing a genetic condition.

Diagnostic tests are typically performed after an individual has shown symptoms of a genetic condition. These tests can be used to identify the specific genetic mutation that is causing the condition, which can help to guide treatment and management. Screening tests, on the other hand, are performed on individuals who do not have any symptoms of a genetic condition. These tests can identify individuals who are at risk for developing a condition, allowing them to take steps to prevent or manage the condition.

Interpreting Test Results

The interpretation of genetic test results is a complex process that requires careful consideration of a variety of factors, including:

The type of test: Diagnostic tests are used to confirm or rule out a specific genetic condition, while screening tests are used to identify individuals who may be at risk for developing a genetic condition.
The individual's personal and family history: This information can help to provide context for the test results and to identify potential risk factors.
The potential implications of the results: The results of genetic tests can have significant implications for an individual's health, reproductive choices, and family planning.

It is important to note that genetic test results are not always definitive. In some cases, the results may be inconclusive or may not provide a clear diagnosis. In these cases, further testing or evaluation may be necessary.

Genetic Counseling

Genetic counseling is a valuable resource for individuals who are considering genetic testing or who have received genetic test results. Genetic counselors are healthcare professionals who have specialized training in genetics and counseling. They can provide information about genetic testing, interpret test results, and help individuals to understand the implications of the results.

Genetic counseling can help individuals to make informed decisions about their health and reproductive choices. It can also provide support and guidance for individuals who are coping with the emotional challenges of genetic testing.

Conclusion

The interpretation of genetic test results is a complex process that requires careful consideration of a variety of factors. It is important to understand the different types of genetic tests, the potential implications of the results, and the role of genetic counseling in the process. By working with a healthcare professional, individuals can make informed decisions about their health and reproductive choices.

134 Benefits and Limitations of Genetic Testing

Genetic testing offers a wealth of potential benefits, including:

Early detection and diagnosis of genetic disorders: Genetic testing can identify genetic mutations associated with various disorders, enabling early detection and diagnosis.

This allows individuals to make informed decisions about their health, such as undergoing preventive measures or seeking appropriate treatment.

Risk assessment for inherited conditions: Genetic testing can estimate the likelihood of developing inherited conditions based on an individual's genetic profile. This information empowers individuals and their families to make informed choices about reproductive planning, lifestyle modifications, and preventative healthcare strategies.

Personalized treatment planning: Genetic testing can provide insights into an individual's unique genetic makeup, allowing healthcare professionals to tailor treatment plans to their specific needs. This personalized approach can optimize treatment efficacy and minimize adverse effects.

Identification of gene-drug interactions: Genetic testing can reveal potential gene-drug interactions, guiding healthcare providers in selecting the most appropriate medications and dosages for each individual.

Research and development of new therapies: Genetic testing contributes to ongoing research efforts, leading to the development of new therapies and treatments for genetic disorders.

Limitations of Genetic Testing

While genetic testing offers numerous advantages, it also has certain limitations:

Incomplete understanding of genetic variants: Our understanding of the human genome is still evolving, and the interpretation of genetic variants can be challenging.

Some variants may have uncertain or variable effects, making it difficult to draw definitive conclusions from genetic testing results.

Psychological impact: Receiving genetic information can have a profound psychological impact on individuals and their families. It is essential to provide appropriate support and counseling to help them cope with the potential emotional and psychological implications of genetic testing.

Privacy and confidentiality concerns: Genetic information is highly sensitive and requires robust measures to ensure privacy and confidentiality. Individuals may be concerned about the potential misuse or discrimination based on their genetic information.

Cost and accessibility: Genetic testing can be expensive, and access to these tests may vary depending on healthcare systems and insurance coverage. This can create disparities in access to genetic testing and limit its benefits for individuals in underserved communities.

Ethical considerations: Genetic testing raises ethical concerns related to reproductive decision-making, informed consent, and the potential for genetic discrimination. It is essential to establish clear guidelines and ethical frameworks to ensure the responsible and equitable use of genetic testing. While it offers numerous benefits, it is crucial to be aware of its limitations and to approach genetic testing with informed decision-making, ethical considerations, and appropriate support systems in place.

Chapter 14: Genetic Enhancement and Modification

141 The Role of Genetic Engineering in Animal Breeding

Genetic engineering, also known as genetic modification or recombinant DNA technology, is a powerful tool that allows scientists to manipulate the genetic material of organisms. This technology has revolutionized the field of animal breeding, enabling the development of animals with desirable traits such as improved growth rates, disease resistance, and enhanced reproductive performance.

Enhancing Production Traits

One of the primary applications of genetic engineering in animal breeding is to enhance production traits. For example, scientists have developed cattle breeds that produce more milk or have leaner meat. Similarly, in poultry, genetic engineering has been used to create chickens that lay more eggs or have larger breasts. These advancements have significantly increased the efficiency of animal production, leading to increased food availability and reduced costs for consumers.

Improving Disease Resistance

Genetic engineering can also be used to improve disease

resistance in animals. By introducing genes that confer resistance to specific diseases, scientists can create animals that are less susceptible to infection. This has been particularly successful in the development of livestock vaccines. For instance, researchers have developed a vaccine for foot-and-mouth disease in cattle, which has significantly reduced the incidence of this devastating disease.

Enhancing Reproductive Performance

Genetic engineering has also been utilized to enhance reproductive performance in animals. For example, scientists have developed pigs that are more fertile and have larger litter sizes. This has the potential to significantly increase the efficiency of pig production and reduce the number of animals required to meet market demand.

Ethical Considerations

While genetic engineering offers numerous potential benefits, it also raises important ethical considerations. One concern is the potential for unintended consequences or harm to animals or the environment. It is crucial to conduct thorough safety assessments and ensure that genetically modified animals are not released into the wild without careful evaluation of potential ecological impacts.

Consumer Acceptance

Another ethical consideration is consumer acceptance. There may be concerns among consumers about the safety and ethical implications of consuming genetically modified animals or animal products. Open and transparent communication about the benefits and risks of genetic engineering is essential for building public trust and acceptance.

Conclusion

Genetic engineering has the potential to revolutionize animal breeding and provide numerous benefits to society. By enhancing production traits, improving disease resistance, and enhancing reproductive performance, genetic engineering can increase the efficiency of animal production and contribute to a more sustainable and secure food supply. However, it is crucial to proceed responsibly, considering the ethical implications and engaging in open and informed dialogue with stakeholders to ensure the safe and responsible use of this powerful technology.

142 Ethical Considerations Regarding Genetic Modification

Genetic modification (GM) has emerged as a transformative technology with the potential to reshape our understanding of biology and its applications in various fields. However, alongside its transformative potential, GM has also sparked significant ethical concerns that warrant careful consideration.

Ethical Considerations

1. Environmental Concerns:
GM can alter the genetic makeup of organisms, including plants and animals. This raises concerns about the potential impact on biodiversity and ecological balance. Some critics argue that GM crops could outcompete native species, disrupt food chains, and contribute to the spread of invasive species. Additionally, the use of GM crops may lead to the

increased use of pesticides and herbicides, which can harm beneficial insects and pollute waterways.

2. Human Health Concerns:
The long-term effects of consuming GM foods on human health are still not fully understood. Some studies have raised concerns about the potential for allergic reactions, antibiotic resistance, and other unintended health consequences. Critics argue that the lack of long-term safety data poses a risk to consumers and that more rigorous testing is necessary before widespread consumption of GM foods.

3. Ethical Challenges Related to Informed Consent:
GM technologies can have profound implications for the genetic heritage of future generations. Critics argue that humans do not have the right to alter the genetic makeup of other organisms, especially those that are passed on to future generations. They believe that GM violates the autonomy and dignity of other species and that future generations should have the right to make decisions about their own genetic makeup.

4. Ownership and Control of Genetic Resources:
GM technologies have the potential to concentrate ownership and control of genetic resources in the hands of a few corporations. Critics argue that this could lead to monopolization of the seed industry, reduced diversity of crops, and increased dependency on proprietary technologies. They emphasize the need for equitable access to genetic resources and the preservation of traditional knowledge systems related to agriculture.

5. Unintended Consequences and the Precautionary Principle:

GM technologies are complex and can have unforeseen consequences. Critics argue that the precautionary principle should be applied when introducing new GM products, especially those intended for widespread use. They believe that it is better to err on the side of caution and conduct thorough risk assessments before releasing GM organisms into the environment or the food supply.

Approaching Ethical Considerations

Addressing the ethical considerations surrounding GM requires a balanced approach that considers both the potential benefits and risks. It is essential to engage in open and transparent dialogue among scientists, policymakers, and the public. Ethical guidelines and regulations should be developed to ensure that GM technologies are used responsibly and in a way that minimizes potential risks.

Role of Values in Decision-Making:

Ethical considerations in GM are often rooted in fundamental values such as environmental stewardship, human well-being, justice, and equity. These values guide our decisions and shape our perspectives on the risks and benefits associated with GM. It is important to acknowledge that different values can lead to different ethical conclusions.

Importance of Public Engagement:

Informed public engagement is crucial for making ethical decisions about GM. Public trust and acceptance of GM technologies depend on transparent information and open dialogue. Governments, scientists, and industry have a responsibility to provide accurate information about GM and to listen to public concerns. By carefully weighing the potential benefits and risks, engaging in open dialogue, and adhering to ethical principles, we can ensure that GM technologies are used in a way that respects human well-being, environmental integrity, and the autonomy of future generations.

143 Potential Benefits and Risks of Genetic Modification in Rabbits

Genetic modification (GM) is a powerful technology that allows scientists to alter the genetic makeup of organisms. This technology has the potential to improve the health and productivity of animals, including rabbits. However, it also raises concerns about the potential risks to animals and the environment.

Potential Benefits of Genetic Modification in Rabbits

GM could provide a number of benefits for rabbits. For example, GM rabbits could be made more resistant to diseases, which would reduce the need for antibiotics and other treatments. GM rabbits could also be made more productive, which would lead to increased meat and fur production. Additionally, GM rabbits could be made to produce valuable proteins or other substances for use in medicine or industry.

Potential Risks of Genetic Modification in Rabbits

There are also potential risks associated with GM in rabbits. One concern is that GM rabbits could escape into the wild and interbreed with wild rabbits, which could lead to the spread of GM genes throughout the population. This could have unintended consequences for wild rabbit populations, such as making them more susceptible to disease or reducing their genetic diversity.

Another concern is that GM rabbits could have unintended health effects. For example, GM rabbits that are made more resistant to one disease could become more susceptible to another disease. Additionally, GM rabbits could develop new allergies or other health problems.

Conclusion

GM is a powerful technology with the potential to improve the health and productivity of rabbits. However, it also raises concerns about the potential risks to animals and the environment. It is important to weigh the potential benefits and risks of GM before making a decision about whether or not to use this technology.

Additional Considerations

In addition to the potential benefits and risks discussed above, there are a number of other factors to consider when evaluating the use of GM in rabbits. These factors include:

The ethical implications of GM. Some people believe that it is wrong to alter the genetic makeup of animals. Others believe that GM is a valuable tool that can be used to improve the lives of animals and humans.
The regulatory environment for GM. The use of GM in animals is regulated by government agencies in many countries. These regulations are designed to protect the health and safety of animals and the environment.
The public perception of GM. There is a great deal of public concern about the use of GM in food and agriculture. It is important to address these concerns and provide the public

with accurate information about GM. It is important to weigh the potential benefits and risks before making a decision about whether or not to use this technology.

144 The Future of Genetic Enhancement in Rabbit Breeding

The advent of genetic engineering and biotechnology has revolutionized the field of animal breeding, and rabbit breeding is no exception. Genetic enhancement techniques offer the potential to improve desirable traits in rabbits, such as growth rate, meat quality, disease resistance, and reproductive performance.

One promising area of genetic enhancement is the use of marker-assisted selection (MAS). This technique utilizes genetic markers linked to specific traits to identify animals with desirable genotypes. By selecting for these markers, breeders can increase the frequency of favorable alleles in their breeding stock, leading to improved performance in subsequent generations.

Another approach is gene editing, which allows scientists to make precise changes to the DNA of an organism. This technology has the potential to correct genetic defects, introduce new traits, or enhance existing ones. For example, gene editing could be used to increase the growth rate of rabbits or improve their resistance to specific diseases.

Transgenic technology involves the introduction of foreign genes into the genome of an organism. This technique has been used to create rabbits with enhanced traits, such as increased muscle mass or resistance to viral infections. However, transgenic technology also raises ethical and regulatory concerns that need to be carefully considered.

Genome-wide association studies (GWAS) are a powerful tool for identifying genetic variants associated with complex traits. By analyzing the genomes of a large number of individuals, researchers can identify genetic markers that influence traits such as growth rate, feed efficiency, and carcass quality. This information can then be used to develop genomic selection tools to predict the genetic merit of breeding animals.

The future of genetic enhancement in rabbit breeding is bright. As technology continues to advance, new and innovative approaches will emerge to improve the genetic potential of rabbits. However, it is important to proceed with caution and ensure that genetic enhancement techniques are used responsibly and ethically.

Here are some specific examples of how genetic enhancement is being used to improve rabbits:

Growth rate: Researchers have identified genetic markers associated with growth rate in rabbits. By selecting for these markers, breeders can increase the average daily gain of their animals, resulting in faster-growing rabbits with higher meat yields.

Meat quality: Genetic enhancement techniques can also be used to improve the meat quality of rabbits. For example, researchers have developed rabbits with higher levels of intramuscular fat, which results in more tender and flavorful meat.

Disease resistance: Genetic enhancement can help to improve the disease resistance of rabbits. For example, researchers have developed rabbits that are resistant to specific diseases, such as viral hemorrhagic disease (VHD) and coccidiosis.

Reproductive performance: Genetic enhancement techniques can also be used to improve the reproductive performance of rabbits. For example, researchers have developed rabbits with increased litter size and reduced embryonic mortality.

The benefits of genetic enhancement in rabbit breeding are clear. By using these techniques, breeders can improve the growth rate, meat quality, disease resistance, and reproductive performance of their animals. This can lead to increased profitability for rabbit producers and improved meat quality for consumers.

However, it is important to note that genetic enhancement also raises some ethical concerns. For example, some people argue that it is unethical to alter the genetic makeup of animals for human benefit. Others worry that genetic enhancement could lead to the creation of "designer animals" that are not adapted to natural environments.

It is important to weigh the potential benefits and risks of genetic enhancement carefully before using these techniques in rabbit breeding. Open and transparent discussions among scientists, breeders, and consumers are essential to ensure that genetic enhancement is used responsibly and ethically. However, it is important to use these techniques responsibly and ethically to ensure that the benefits outweigh the risks. With careful planning and oversight, genetic enhancement can help to create a more sustainable and productive rabbit breeding industry.

Chapter 15: The Impact of Genetics on Rabbit Behavior

151 Understanding the Genetic Basis of Rabbit Behavior

Genetics provides the blueprint for an animal's physical and behavioral traits, while the environment shapes how these traits are expressed. Understanding the genetic basis of rabbit behavior is crucial for breeders, veterinarians, and researchers alike, as it can help them predict and modify behaviors, improve breeding programs, and diagnose and treat behavioral disorders.

The Role of Genes in Rabbit Behavior

Genes are the units of heredity that carry the instructions for an organism's development and function. Each gene contains a specific DNA sequence that encodes for a particular protein. Proteins are the building blocks of cells and tissues and play a vital role in all aspects of an animal's physiology, including behavior.

The genetic basis of rabbit behavior is polygenic, meaning that multiple genes are involved in determining a particular trait. These genes can be located on different chromosomes or on the same chromosome. The interaction of these genes, as well as their interaction with the environment, determines the final expression of a behavior.

Genetic Variation in Rabbit Behavior

There is a wide range of genetic variation in rabbit behavior, both within and between breeds. This variation is due to mutations, which are changes in the DNA sequence. Mutations can be spontaneous or induced by environmental factors.

Selective breeding has been used for centuries to enhance desirable behaviors in rabbits. Breeders have selected for rabbits that exhibit specific traits, such as tameness, docility, or productivity. This process has led to the development of distinct breeds, each with its own unique behavioral characteristics.

Behavioral Genetics Research in Rabbits

Behavioral genetics research in rabbits has identified several genes that are associated with specific behaviors. For example, the agouti gene has been linked to tameness, while the albino gene has been linked to increased fearfulness.

Quantitative trait locus (QTL) mapping studies have been used to identify regions of the genome that are associated with complex behavioral traits, such as aggression and maternal behavior. QTL mapping involves identifying genetic markers that are linked to a particular trait and then using statistical methods to map the location of the gene responsible for the trait.

Implications for Rabbit Breeders and Veterinarians

Understanding the genetic basis of rabbit behavior has important implications for rabbit breeders and veterinarians.

Breeders can use genetic information to select for rabbits that exhibit desirable behaviors, such as tameness and docility. This can help to improve the overall quality of rabbit stock and reduce the incidence of behavioral problems.

Veterinarians can use genetic information to diagnose and treat behavioral disorders in rabbits. By understanding the genetic basis of a particular disorder, veterinarians can develop more effective treatment strategies.

Future Directions in Rabbit Behavioral Genetics

The field of rabbit behavioral genetics is still in its early stages. However, ongoing research is providing valuable insights into the genetic basis of rabbit behavior. Future research will focus on identifying additional genes that are associated with specific behaviors, understanding the interaction of genes and the environment, and developing genetic tests for behavioral traits.

Conclusion

The genetic basis of rabbit behavior is complex and involves the interaction of multiple genes and the environment. Understanding this genetic basis is crucial for breeders, veterinarians, and researchers alike. By harnessing the power of genetics, we can improve the overall quality of rabbit stock, reduce the incidence of behavioral problems, and better understand the nature of rabbit behavior.

152 Identifying Genetic Traits Associated with Temperament

Understanding the genetic basis of temperament is crucial for unraveling the intricate interplay between nature and nurture in shaping our personality. This one delves into the methods and challenges involved in identifying genetic traits associated with temperament, shedding light on the complex relationship between genes and behavior.

Quantitative Trait Loci (QTL) Analysis

One approach to identifying genetic traits linked to temperament is Quantitative Trait Loci (QTL) analysis. QTLs are specific regions of the genome associated with variations in a quantitative trait, such as temperament. By comparing the DNA of individuals with varying temperamental traits, researchers can identify genomic regions that may harbor genes influencing temperament. QTL analysis has been successful in identifying candidate genes for temperament in both humans and animal models.

Genome-Wide Association Studies (GWAS)

Genome-Wide Association Studies (GWAS) are a powerful tool for identifying genetic variants associated with complex traits like temperament. GWAS analyze hundreds of thousands of genetic markers across the entire genome, searching for variations that are more common in individuals with specific temperamental characteristics. By comparing the genetic profiles of large sample sizes, GWAS can identify genetic variants that contribute to individual differences in temperament.

Candidate Gene Studies

Candidate gene studies focus on specific genes that are hypothesized to play a role in temperament based on their known functions or associations with related traits. Researchers select candidate genes based on prior research, physiological mechanisms, or evolutionary considerations. By examining variations within these candidate genes, researchers can investigate their potential role in shaping temperamental traits.

Challenges in Identifying Genetic Traits

Identifying genetic traits associated with temperament is a challenging task due to the complex nature of temperament and the multifaceted interplay of genetic and environmental factors. Some of the challenges include:

Sample size: Genetic studies require large sample sizes to achieve statistical power and minimize the influence of confounding factors. Gathering sufficiently large samples with reliable temperament assessments can be challenging. Genetic heterogeneity: Temperament is a complex trait likely influenced by multiple genes, each contributing small effects. This genetic heterogeneity makes it difficult to pinpoint specific genetic variants responsible for temperament variations.
Environmental interactions: Temperament is not solely determined by genetics. Environmental factors, such as early experiences and socialization, can significantly influence its development. Identifying genetic effects in the presence of environmental influences is a complex task.

Significance and Implications

Identifying genetic traits associated with temperament has significant implications for understanding human behavior and developing personalized approaches to mental health. By unraveling the genetic underpinnings of temperament, researchers can:

Improve diagnostic accuracy: Genetic markers can provide additional information to aid in the diagnosis of temperament-related disorders and conditions.
Develop targeted interventions: Understanding the genetic basis of temperament can inform the development of tailored interventions that capitalize on individual strengths and address potential vulnerabilities.
Advance personalized medicine: Genetic information can guide personalized treatments by predicting treatment response and identifying individuals at risk for developing temperamental disorders.

Conclusion

Identifying genetic traits associated with temperament is a complex and ongoing endeavor. By employing advanced genetic analysis techniques and leveraging large sample sizes, researchers are gradually uncovering the genetic underpinnings of this fundamental aspect of human psychology. Understanding the genetic basis of temperament holds promise for improving diagnostic accuracy, developing targeted interventions, and advancing personalized medicine. However, it is essential to approach this research with caution, considering the complexity of genetic-environmental interactions and the potential ethical implications of using genetic information for behavioral prediction and treatment.

153 The Role of Genetics in Training and Handling Rabbits

The field of genetics plays a significant role in the effective training and handling of rabbits. Understanding the genetic predispositions and traits of different rabbit breeds can provide valuable insights into their trainability, temperament, and behavioral tendencies.

Breed-Specific Characteristics

Different rabbit breeds exhibit distinct genetic traits that influence their suitability for various training and handling purposes. For instance, breeds like the Mini Lop and Holland Lop are renowned for their docile and affectionate nature, making them ideal for companionship and indoor environments. Conversely, breeds like the Flemish Giant and New Zealand White are known for their larger size and more active temperaments, which may require more rigorous training and handling techniques.

Temperament and Trainability

The genetic makeup of rabbits influences their temperament and trainability. Some breeds, such as the Californian and Silver Fox, are naturally more curious and receptive to training, exhibiting a willingness to learn new behaviors. Others, like the Dwarf Hotot and English Angora, may be more independent and require a gentler, more patient approach to training.

Behavioral Tendencies

Genetics also plays a role in shaping the behavioral tendencies of rabbits. For example, breeds like the Rex and Satin are known for their playful and energetic nature, while breeds like the American Fuzzy Lop and Lionhead tend to be more laid-back and relaxed. Understanding these behavioral tendencies can help handlers tailor their training and handling methods accordingly.

Responsible Breeding

Responsible breeding practices are essential to ensure the genetic health and well-being of rabbits. Breeders should carefully select breeding pairs based on their desired traits, considering both physical and behavioral characteristics. By maintaining genetic diversity and avoiding inbreeding, breeders can help preserve the unique qualities of each breed while minimizing the risk of inherited health conditions.

Implications for Training

Knowledge of rabbit genetics can greatly enhance the effectiveness of training and handling efforts. By understanding the genetic predispositions of a particular rabbit, handlers can adjust their training methods to suit its temperament and trainability. For example, breeds that are naturally more curious and eager to please may respond well to positive reinforcement and reward-based training, while more independent breeds may require a more consistent and structured approach.

Ethical Considerations

The use of genetics in rabbit training and handling raises important ethical considerations. It is crucial to approach genetic selection and breeding practices with a responsible and humane mindset, ensuring the well-being and happiness of the rabbits involved. Breeders and handlers should prioritize the preservation of genetic diversity and avoid practices that could lead to the development of undesirable or harmful traits.

Conclusion

The field of genetics offers valuable insights into the training and handling of rabbits. By understanding the breed-specific characteristics, temperament, trainability, behavioral tendencies, and responsible breeding practices associated with different rabbit breeds, handlers can tailor their approaches to maximize the effectiveness of training and ensure the well-being of these captivating companions.

154 Breeding for Desirable Behavioral Characteristics

The realm of animal breeding encompasses not only physical traits but also behavioral characteristics. Behavior, a complex interplay of genetic and environmental factors, can significantly influence an animal's adaptability, productivity, and welfare. Understanding the genetic basis of behavior is paramount for breeders seeking to enhance desirable traits in their livestock.

Genetic Basis of Behavior

Behavior is a multifaceted phenomenon influenced by multiple genes, each contributing to specific aspects of an animal's temperament, learning abilities, and social interactions. Genetic variants, known as alleles, at different gene loci can give rise to variations in behavioral traits. For instance, in dogs, the serotonin transporter gene (SLC6A4) has been linked to aggression and fearfulness.

Quantitative Genetics

The genetic inheritance of behavioral traits often follows a quantitative pattern, meaning that multiple genes contribute to the trait's expression. Quantitative genetics provides a framework for analyzing the genetic basis of complex traits. Heritability, a measure of the proportion of phenotypic variation attributable to genetic factors, is estimated using statistical methods. High heritability indicates a stronger genetic influence on the trait, while low heritability suggests a greater environmental influence.

Breeding for Behavioral Traits

Selective breeding, a cornerstone of animal breeding, involves mating individuals with desirable traits to produce offspring with similar characteristics. In the context of behavioral traits, breeders can select animals that exhibit desired behaviors and exclude those with undesirable ones. This approach, known as mass selection, has been successfully employed to improve behavioral traits in various livestock species.

Challenges in Breeding for Behavior

Breeding for behavioral traits poses unique challenges compared to physical traits. Measuring and quantifying behavior can be subjective and prone to observer bias. Furthermore, behavioral traits are often influenced by environmental factors, making it difficult to isolate genetic effects. Additionally, ethical considerations arise when selecting for specific behaviors, as some traits may have unintended consequences on animal welfare.

Non-Genetic Factors Influencing Behavior

While genetics plays a significant role in shaping behavior, environmental factors also exert a profound influence. Nutrition, housing conditions, early experiences, and social interactions can all impact an animal's behavioral development and expression. Breeders must consider these factors and implement management practices that optimize the environment for desired behaviors.

Emerging Technologies in Behavioral Genetics

Advancements in genetic technologies, such as genome-wide association studies (GWAS), are providing valuable insights into the genetic basis of behavior. GWAS identify genomic regions associated with specific behavioral traits, facilitating the development of genetic markers for use in selective breeding programs. Additionally, epigenetic research explores how environmental factors can alter gene expression, potentially influencing behavioral traits.

Conclusion

Breeding for desirable behavioral characteristics is a complex yet rewarding endeavor. By understanding the genetic basis of behavior, employing quantitative genetic principles, and carefully considering environmental factors, breeders can make informed decisions to enhance the behavioral traits of their livestock. Ongoing research and technological advancements continue to refine our understanding of behavioral genetics, paving the way for further improvements in animal breeding and welfare.

Chapter 16: The Role of Nutrition in Genetics

161 The Interaction Between Genetics and Nutrition

In the past, the focus of nutritional research primarily centered around the macronutrient and micronutrient composition of food and its impact on physiological processes. However, advancements in genetic technologies have illuminated the critical role that genetic variations play in modulating an individual's response to dietary interventions. This emerging field, known as nutrigenetics, explores the complex relationship between genetic makeup and nutritional requirements, paving the way for personalized nutrition approaches.

Genetic Influences on Nutrient Metabolism

Our genetic endowment exerts a significant influence on how we metabolize and utilize nutrients. Specific gene variants can alter the activity of enzymes involved in nutrient absorption, transport, and utilization, affecting the bioavailability and biological effects of dietary components. For instance, genetic variations in the lactase gene can lead to lactose intolerance, an inability to digest the sugar found in milk. Similarly, genetic polymorphisms in the folate metabolism pathway can impact folate absorption and utilization, potentially increasing the risk of neural tube defects in offspring.

Personalized Nutrition and Disease Susceptibility

Nutrigenetics has significant implications for personalized nutrition, enabling tailored dietary recommendations based on an individual's genetic profile. By identifying genetic variants associated with increased susceptibility to certain chronic diseases, such as obesity, diabetes, and cardiovascular disease, healthcare professionals can provide personalized dietary guidance aimed at reducing disease risk. For example, individuals with a genetic predisposition to obesity may benefit from personalized diets that emphasize weight management and minimize inflammation.

Nutrient-Gene Interactions and Health Outcomes

Beyond the direct effects of genetic variation on nutrient metabolism, there is growing evidence of nutrient-gene interactions that influence health outcomes. Certain nutrients can modulate gene expression and alter the activity of specific genes. For instance, research suggests that dietary intake of omega-3 fatty acids can influence the expression of genes involved in inflammation and cardiovascular health. Moreover, the timing and duration of nutritional interventions can also impact the effectiveness of genetic interventions.

Challenges and Future Directions

Despite the tremendous potential of nutrigenetics, several challenges remain. The complex nature of gene-nutrient interactions and the variability in genetic profiles pose significant hurdles in translating research findings into practical applications. Additionally, the cost and accessibility of genetic testing can limit its widespread adoption. Future research endeavors should focus on elucidating the mechanisms underlying gene-nutrient interactions, developing reliable and cost-effective genetic testing methods, and establishing evidence-based guidelines for personalized nutrition interventions.

Conclusion

The interaction between genetics and nutrition is a rapidly evolving field that offers promising opportunities to improve human health. By understanding the genetic basis of nutrient metabolism and its implications for disease susceptibility, healthcare professionals can tailor dietary recommendations to meet individual needs. As research progresses, we can anticipate further advancements in personalized nutrition, leading to more effective and individualized approaches to disease prevention and management.

162 The Impact of Diet on Genetic Expression

At the core of this field lies the fundamental understanding that the foods we consume can exert profound effects on our genetic makeup, influencing the way our genes are expressed and ultimately shaping our health and well-being.

Epigenetics and Gene Expression

To fully comprehend the impact of diet on genetic expression, we must delve into the realm of epigenetics. Epigenetics refers to the heritable changes in gene expression that occur without altering the underlying DNA sequence. These changes can be influenced by various environmental factors, including diet.

One of the primary mechanisms through which diet modulates gene expression is via DNA methylation. DNA methylation involves the addition of methyl groups to the DNA molecule, which can either suppress or enhance gene expression. For instance, a high intake of folate, a B vitamin found in leafy green vegetables, has been associated with decreased DNA methylation of genes involved in cancer development. Conversely, a diet rich in saturated fats has been linked to increased DNA methylation of genes related to cardiovascular disease.

Nutritional Epigenetics

The emerging field of nutritional epigenetics seeks to elucidate the specific dietary components that influence epigenetic modifications and their subsequent impact on gene expression. Studies have demonstrated that certain nutrients, such as vitamins, minerals, and phytochemicals, can act as epigenetic modulators, altering DNA methylation patterns and histone modifications.

For example, research has shown that a diet high in polyphenols, found in fruits and vegetables, can promote global DNA hypomethylation, a state associated with increased gene expression. On the other hand, a diet low in choline, an essential nutrient found in eggs and liver, has been linked to increased DNA methylation of genes involved in neural development.

Dietary Influences on Gene Expression

The impact of diet on gene expression extends beyond

epigenetic modifications. Nutrients can also directly interact with transcription factors, proteins that regulate gene expression. For instance, vitamin D, which is obtained from sunlight and certain foods, acts as a transcription factor, binding to specific DNA sequences and promoting gene expression.

Moreover, dietary components can alter the expression of microRNAs (miRNAs), small non-coding RNA molecules that play a crucial role in gene regulation. miRNAs bind to messenger RNA (mRNA), the intermediary molecule between DNA and protein synthesis, and can either block translation or promote its degradation. Studies have shown that a diet high in fruits and vegetables can increase the expression of miRNAs involved in cancer prevention, while a diet high in processed foods can decrease the expression of these protective miRNAs.

Implications for Health and Disease

The understanding of how diet influences genetic expression has profound implications for our health. By optimizing our dietary intake, we can potentially modify our epigenetic landscape and reduce our risk of chronic diseases such as cancer, cardiovascular disease, and neurodegenerative disorders.

For instance, a Mediterranean-style diet, which is rich in fruits, vegetables, whole grains, and lean protein, has been associated with a reduced risk of cardiovascular disease and certain types of cancer. This protective effect is attributed, in part, to the diet's ability to modulate gene expression, including the upregulation of genes involved in anti-inflammatory and antioxidant pathways.

Conclusion

The field of nutrigenomics has unveiled the profound impact of diet on genetic expression. Through epigenetic modifications, nutrient-gene interactions, and the regulation of miRNAs, diet can influence the way our genes are expressed, shaping our health and disease susceptibility. By embracing a nutrient-rich, balanced diet, we can harness the power of nutrition to optimize our genetic potential and promote optimal health and well-being.

163 Optimizing Nutrition for Genetic Potential

It is now recognized that our genetic makeup plays a significant role in determining our nutritional needs and responses to different dietary components. By optimizing our nutrition based on our genetic potential, we can maximize our health outcomes and reduce the risk of developing chronic diseases.

Genetic Variation and Nutritional Needs

Our genetic code contains variations that influence various aspects of metabolism, including nutrient absorption, utilization, and excretion. These variations can impact our requirements for specific nutrients, such as vitamins, minerals, and macronutrients (carbohydrates, proteins, and fats). For example, some genetic variants may lead to reduced absorption of certain vitamins, such as vitamin D, or increased susceptibility to nutrient deficiencies.

Personalized Nutrition

Nutrigenomics enables the development of personalized nutrition plans that are tailored to an individual's genetic profile. By analyzing an individual's DNA, healthcare professionals can identify genetic variants that may affect their nutritional needs and provide recommendations accordingly. This approach can help prevent nutrient deficiencies, optimize metabolic function, and reduce the risk of chronic diseases associated with poor nutrition.

Examples of Genetic-Based Nutritional Recommendations

Vitamin D: Individuals with genetic variants that impair vitamin D absorption may require higher dietary intake or supplementation.
Folate: Genetic variations in folate metabolism can affect the body's ability to utilize this essential nutrient, which may necessitate increased dietary folate intake.
Caffeine: Genetic variants influence caffeine metabolism, with some individuals experiencing increased sensitivity or tolerance to caffeine.
Sodium: Genetic variations in blood pressure regulation can affect an individual's susceptibility to sodium-induced hypertension.
Alcohol: Genetic variants can influence alcohol metabolism, affecting an individual's risk of alcohol-related liver disease.

Implementation of Nutrigenomics in Practice

The implementation of nutrigenomics in clinical practice is still in its early stages but is rapidly evolving. Several genetic tests are available to assess genetic variants related to nutrition. Healthcare professionals can use the results of these tests to provide personalized nutrition guidance and optimize patient care.

Benefits of Optimizing Nutrition for Genetic Potential

Improved health outcomes: Optimizing nutrition based on genetic potential can help prevent nutrient deficiencies, improve metabolic function, and reduce the risk of chronic diseases, such as cardiovascular disease, diabetes, and certain types of cancer.
Personalized nutrition plans: Nutrigenomics enables the development of tailored nutrition plans that are specifically designed to meet an individual's unique genetic needs.
Enhanced disease management: By understanding the genetic basis of nutritional requirements, healthcare professionals can provide more effective dietary recommendations for individuals with specific health conditions.

Conclusion

Optimizing nutrition for genetic potential is a groundbreaking approach that has the potential to transform healthcare. By leveraging the power of nutrigenomics, we can tailor our dietary choices to meet our individual genetic needs, maximize our health outcomes, and reduce the risk of chronic diseases. As research in this field continues to expand, we can expect further advancements and a deeper understanding of the complex relationship between nutrition and genetics.

164 Understanding the Genetic Basis of Nutritional Needs

The field of nutrigenetics, which examines the interplay between genetics and nutrition, has gained significant momentum in recent years. It delves into how genetic variations influence an individual's nutritional requirements and susceptibility to nutrition-related diseases. By understanding these genetic underpinnings, we can tailor dietary recommendations to optimize health outcomes.

Genetic Polymorphisms and Nutrient Metabolism

Genetic polymorphisms are variations in DNA sequences that can affect gene function. These polymorphisms can influence nutrient metabolism, absorption, and utilization. For instance, polymorphisms in the MTHFR gene, involved in folate metabolism, can impact folate bioavailability and increase the risk of neural tube defects in infants.

Similarly, variations in the APOE gene, which encodes a cholesterol transport protein, are associated with differential responses to dietary fats. Individuals with certain APOE genotypes may exhibit altered lipid metabolism and a higher susceptibility to cardiovascular disease.

Personalized Nutrition

The concept of personalized nutrition, tailored to an individual's genetic profile, is gaining traction. Genetic testing can identify specific polymorphisms that influence nutrient needs and disease risk. This information can guide dietary recommendations, ensuring that individuals receive the optimal balance of nutrients for their unique genetic makeup.

For example, individuals with genetic variants that impair folate metabolism may require higher intakes of folate-rich foods or fortified supplements to mitigate the risk of neural tube defects. Similarly, those with APOE genotypes associated with increased cardiovascular risk may benefit from dietary strategies that reduce saturated fat intake and promote heart-healthy fats.

Dietary Guidelines and Nutrigenetics

Current dietary guidelines provide general recommendations based on population averages. However, nutrigenetics has the potential to refine these guidelines and make them more precise for individuals with specific genetic predispositions. By considering genetic variations, dietary recommendations can be customized to address individual nutrient needs and reduce the risk of chronic diseases.

Ethical Considerations

While nutrigenetics offers promising opportunities for personalized nutrition, it also raises ethical considerations. The potential misuse of genetic information, privacy concerns, and the need for informed consent are important issues to address. Ethical guidelines must be established to ensure that genetic testing for nutritional purposes is conducted responsibly and in a manner that respects individuals' rights and well-being.

Future Directions

The field of nutrigenetics is still in its infancy, but it holds immense potential for revolutionizing the way we approach nutrition and health. As research continues, we will gain a deeper understanding of the genetic basis of nutritional needs and develop more effective personalized nutrition strategies. This will empower individuals to make informed dietary choices based on their unique genetic blueprint, leading to improved health outcomes and a reduction in chronic disease risk.

Chapter 17: Genetic Resources and Online Tools

171 Accessing Genetic Information and Resources

The advent of genomic technologies has revolutionized our understanding of human health and disease. The ability to sequence and analyze an individual's genome has opened up unprecedented opportunities for personalized medicine, where treatment decisions can be tailored to each patient's unique genetic makeup. However, accessing and interpreting genetic information can be a complex and challenging process.

Sources of Genetic Information

There are several sources from which individuals can obtain their genetic information:

Clinical Genetic Testing: Performed by healthcare professionals to diagnose or predict the risk of genetic disorders. Samples are typically obtained through blood or saliva.
Direct-to-Consumer Genetic Testing: Companies like 23andMe and AncestryDNA offer genetic testing kits that allow individuals to learn about their ancestry, health risks, and genetic traits.
Biobanks: Collections of biological samples and associated

data, including genetic information, that are used for research purposes.

Accessing Genetic Information

Accessing genetic information can be done through various channels:

Medical Records: If individuals have undergone clinical genetic testing, their results will be documented in their medical records.
Genetic Counselors: Healthcare professionals who provide information and support to individuals considering genetic testing or who have received genetic results.
Direct-to-Consumer Genetic Testing Companies: Individuals can order genetic testing kits online and receive their results directly.

Interpreting Genetic Information

Interpreting genetic information can be challenging, as many genetic variants have complex and uncertain implications. It is important to seek professional guidance from a genetic counselor or healthcare provider to understand the implications of genetic results.

Genetic Variants: Genetic information is composed of genetic variants, which are differences in DNA sequences. Some variants are common and benign, while others are rare and may be associated with increased risk of disease.
Risk Assessment: Genetic testing can provide information about an individual's risk of developing certain diseases. However, it is important to remember that genetic risk is only a probability and does not guarantee that a disease will develop.

Personalized Treatment: Genetic information can guide treatment decisions by identifying the most effective and safest medications for an individual based on their genetic makeup.

Ethical Considerations

Accessing genetic information raises important ethical considerations:

Privacy: Genetic information is highly personal and sensitive. It is important to ensure that individuals have control over how their genetic information is used and disclosed.
Discrimination: Genetic information could be used to discriminate against individuals in employment, insurance, and other areas. It is crucial to have laws and regulations in place to protect individuals from genetic discrimination.
Psychological Impact: Genetic information can have a significant impact on an individual's self-concept and emotional well-being. It is essential to provide individuals with appropriate support and resources to cope with the implications of their genetic results.

Conclusion

Accessing genetic information can be a transformative experience, providing individuals with insights into their health and ancestry. However, it is important to approach genetic testing with caution and seek professional guidance to ensure that information is interpreted and used appropriately. By carefully navigating the ethical considerations, individuals can harness the power of genetic information to make informed decisions about their health and well-being.

172 Using Online Databases and Tools for Rabbit Breeders

The internet is a vast and ever-expanding resource that can be a valuable tool for rabbit breeders. There are a number of online databases and tools that can help breeders manage their breeding programs, track their rabbits' health and performance, and connect with other breeders.

One of the most popular online databases for rabbit breeders is the American Rabbit Breeders Association (ARBA) database. The ARBA database contains information on all of the rabbits that have been registered with the ARBA, including their pedigrees, show records, and health records. Breeders can use the ARBA database to research potential breeding stock, track the performance of their own rabbits, and identify rabbits that may be carriers of genetic diseases.

Another popular online database for rabbit breeders is the National Rabbit Breeders Association (NRBA) database. The NRBA database contains information on all of the rabbits that have been registered with the NRBA, including their pedigrees, show records, and health records. Breeders can use the NRBA database to research potential breeding stock, track the performance of their own rabbits, and identify rabbits that may be carriers of genetic diseases.

In addition to online databases, there are a number of online tools that can be useful for rabbit breeders. These tools include calculators that can help breeders determine the breeding coefficient of their rabbits, software programs that can help breeders manage their breeding programs, and online forums where breeders can connect with each other and share information.

Calculators

There are a number of online calculators that can help rabbit breeders determine the breeding coefficient of their rabbits. The breeding coefficient is a measure of how closely related two rabbits are. The higher the breeding coefficient, the more closely related the rabbits are. Breeders should avoid breeding rabbits that have a high breeding coefficient, as this can increase the risk of genetic problems.

One popular online calculator for determining the breeding coefficient of rabbits is the RABBITCALC calculator. The RABBITCALC calculator is a free online calculator that can be used to calculate the breeding coefficient of two rabbits based on their pedigrees.

Software Programs

There are a number of software programs that can help rabbit breeders manage their breeding programs. These programs can help breeders keep track of their rabbits' breeding records, health records, and show records. Some of the most popular software programs for rabbit breeders include:

Rabbit Pro
Rabbit Manager
Rabbitry Manager

Online Forums

There are a number of online forums where rabbit breeders can connect with each other and share information. These forums can be a valuable resource for breeders who are looking for advice on breeding, health, or showmanship. Some of the most popular online forums for rabbit breeders include:

Rabbit Talk
The Rabbit Hole
Rabbit Breeders United

The internet can be a valuable tool for rabbit breeders. By using online databases and tools, breeders can manage their breeding programs more effectively, track their rabbits' health and performance, and connect with other breeders.

173 Finding Information on Specific Genetic Traits

The advent of genomic sequencing technologies has revolutionized the field of genetics, making it possible to identify and study specific genetic traits with unprecedented precision. This has led to a wealth of information becoming available on the genetic basis of various traits, diseases, and conditions. However, navigating the vast amount of genetic information can be a daunting task, especially for individuals without a background in genetics.

Online Databases and Resources

One of the primary resources for finding information on specific genetic traits is online databases. These databases compile and curate genetic information from various sources, including scientific studies, research institutions, and clinical laboratories. Some of the most comprehensive and widely used genetic databases include:

National Library of Medicine's (NLM) Genetic Information Resource (GIR): GIR is a comprehensive database that provides access to a wide range of genetic information, including gene sequences, variant annotations, and links to relevant scientific literature.

National Human Genome Research Institute's (NHGRI) Genome Data Viewer: This interactive database allows users to explore the human genome and search for specific genes or genetic variants.

Online Mendelian Inheritance in Man (OMIM): OMIM is a catalog of human genes and genetic disorders that provides detailed information on their inheritance patterns, clinical features, and genetic variants associated with each condition.

Scientific Literature

Another valuable source of information on specific genetic traits is the scientific literature. PubMed, a database maintained by the NLM, provides access to millions of scientific articles, including those related to genetics. By using specific search terms and filters, users can retrieve articles that focus on specific genes, genetic variants, or traits of interest.

Clinical Laboratories

Clinical laboratories offer genetic testing services to diagnose and predict the risk of genetic disorders. These laboratories can provide information on the genetic variants associated with specific traits and conditions. Individuals can consult with their healthcare providers or genetic counselors to determine if genetic testing is appropriate for their specific situation.

Educational Resources

Various educational resources are available to help individuals understand genetic information and its implications. These resources include:

National Human Genome Research Institute (NHGRI) Genetics Home Reference: This website provides user-friendly explanations of genetic concepts, genetic testing, and genetic disorders.
Centers for Disease Control and Prevention (CDC) Learn Genetics: This website offers interactive tutorials, videos, and articles on various aspects of genetics, including genetic traits and genetic counseling.
Genetic Alliance: This organization provides information and support to individuals and families affected by genetic disorders.

Interpretive Services

Interpreting genetic information can be complex, especially for individuals without a background in genetics. Genetic counselors are healthcare professionals who specialize in providing information, counseling, and support to individuals and families affected by genetic conditions. They can help individuals understand the genetic basis of their traits, assess the risks of developing genetic disorders, and make informed decisions about genetic testing and management.

Additional Tips

When searching for information on specific genetic traits, it is important to:

Use specific and accurate search terms.
Consult multiple sources to obtain a comprehensive understanding.
Be aware of the limitations of genetic information and its potential implications.
Seek guidance from healthcare professionals or genetic counselors for interpretation and counseling.

174 Networking with Other Rabbit Breeders and Geneticists

The pursuit of excellence in rabbit breeding and genetics demands an unwavering commitment to continuous learning and collaboration. Establishing a strong network of connections with fellow breeders and geneticists serves as an invaluable resource, offering a wealth of knowledge, support, and inspiration.

Networking provides a platform for exchanging ideas, sharing experiences, and staying abreast of the latest advancements in the field. By engaging with other breeders, you gain access to a collective pool of expertise, fostering a sense of community and mutual support. Through interactions at rabbit shows, industry conferences, and online forums, you can connect with individuals who share your passion for rabbitry.

These connections can facilitate access to breeding stock with desirable traits, allowing you to improve the genetic quality of your rabbits. The exchange of genetic material between breeders promotes genetic diversity and reduces the risk of inbreeding. By collaborating with geneticists, you can gain insights into the genetic makeup of your rabbits, enabling you to make informed breeding decisions.

Networking also presents opportunities for learning and personal growth. Attending workshops, seminars, and lectures conducted by experienced breeders and geneticists allows you to expand your knowledge base and hone your skills. Participating in discussions and sharing your own experiences contributes to a vibrant exchange of ideas, fostering innovation and progress within the rabbitry community.

Beyond the practical benefits, networking plays a crucial role in building a sense of belonging and camaraderie among rabbit enthusiasts. Sharing successes, discussing challenges, and engaging in friendly competition create a supportive and encouraging environment. The bonds forged through these connections extend beyond the realm of rabbitry, fostering lifelong friendships and a shared passion for the animals that bring us together.

In today's digital age, online platforms have emerged as powerful tools for networking. Social media groups, online forums, and dedicated websites provide a convenient and accessible means to connect with fellow breeders from around the world. These virtual communities offer a wealth of information, resources, and opportunities for interaction, supplementing in-person networking efforts.

By actively engaging in networking activities, rabbit breeders and geneticists can cultivate a thriving and interconnected community. The collective knowledge, support, and inspiration derived from these connections empower individuals to achieve greater success in their breeding endeavors, contributing to the advancement of rabbitry as a whole.

Chapter 18: Conclusion: Applying Genetics for Successful Rabbit Breeding

181 Summary of Key Genetic Principles

Genetics is the study of heredity and variation in living organisms. It is a complex field with a rich history, but there are a few key principles that can help you understand the basics.

1. Genes are the units of heredity.

Genes are segments of DNA that code for proteins. Proteins are the building blocks of cells, and they play a vital role in all aspects of life, from metabolism to reproduction.

2. Genes are passed down from parents to offspring.

Each parent contributes one copy of each gene to their offspring. This means that each offspring has two copies of each gene, one from each parent.

3. Genes can be dominant or recessive.

A dominant gene is a gene that is expressed in an individual even if they only have one copy of the gene. A recessive gene is a gene that is only expressed in an individual if they have two copies of the gene.

4. Alleles are different forms of a gene.

Different alleles of a gene can code for different versions of a protein. For example, one allele of the gene for eye color may code for brown eyes, while another allele of the same gene may code for blue eyes.

5. Genotype and phenotype

Genotype refers to the genetic makeup of an individual. It is determined by the alleles that the individual has for each gene.
Phenotype refers to the observable characteristics of an individual. It is determined by the genotype of the individual and by environmental factors.

6. Variation is the raw material for evolution.

Genetic variation is the presence of differences in the genetic makeup of individuals within a population. This variation is the raw material for evolution, which is the process by which populations of organisms change over time.

7. Genetic disorders are caused by mutations.

Mutations are changes in the DNA sequence of a gene. Mutations can be harmful, beneficial, or neutral. Harmful mutations can cause genetic disorders, such as sickle cell anemia and cystic fibrosis.

8. Genetic engineering is the process of altering the DNA of an organism.

Genetic engineering can be used to improve crop yields, create new medicines, and develop new therapies for genetic disorders.

9. Genomics is the study of the entire genome of an organism.

Genomics is a rapidly growing field that is providing new insights into the biology of organisms. Genomics can be used to identify genes, study gene expression, and diagnose genetic disorders.

These are just a few of the key principles of genetics. By understanding these principles, you can gain a better understanding of the world around you.

Additional Resources:

[National Human Genome Research Institute](https:. . www. genome. gov.)
[Genetics Home Reference](https:. . ghr. nlm. nih. gov.)
[American Society of Human Genetics](https:. . www. ashg. org.)

182 Practical Applications of Genetics in Rabbit Breeding

Genetics plays a pivotal role in the field of rabbit breeding, enabling breeders to harness the power of heredity to enhance desirable traits and eliminate undesirable ones. Selective breeding, the cornerstone of genetic improvement in rabbits, involves the controlled mating of individuals with specific genetic characteristics to produce offspring with predictable traits.

Selective Breeding for Improved Meat Production

One of the primary applications of genetics in rabbit breeding is the selection of individuals with superior meat production traits. Breeders focus on characteristics such as growth rate, feed conversion ratio, and carcass quality. By selecting rabbits with high growth rates and efficient feed conversion, breeders can increase meat yield and reduce production costs. Additionally, selecting for favorable carcass traits, such as meatiness and tenderness, enhances the marketability of rabbit meat.

Genetic Enhancement of Fiber Production

Genetics also plays a significant role in improving fiber production in rabbits. Breeders select individuals with desirable fiber characteristics, including length, fineness, and luster. By selectively mating rabbits with superior fiber traits, breeders can develop strains with high-quality wool or angora fiber. The resulting fiber can be used for a variety of purposes, such as yarn production, textiles, and insulation.

Disease Resistance and Health Management

Genetic selection can also enhance the health and disease resistance of rabbit populations. By identifying individuals with natural resistance to specific diseases, breeders can incorporate these traits into their breeding programs. This approach reduces the incidence of disease outbreaks, lowers mortality rates, and improves overall animal welfare. Additionally, genetic markers can be used to identify carriers of genetic diseases, enabling breeders to eliminate these traits from their breeding stock.

Preservation of Genetic Diversity

Genetic diversity is crucial for the long-term sustainability of rabbit breeding. By maintaining a wide genetic base, breeders can reduce the risk of inbreeding and the associated problems of genetic drift and loss of vigor. Genetic conservation programs aim to preserve the genetic diversity of rare or endangered rabbit breeds, ensuring their availability for future breeding and research purposes.

Genetic Engineering and Biotechnology

Advancements in genetic engineering and biotechnology offer new possibilities for genetic improvement in rabbit breeding. Techniques such as gene editing and transgenesis can be used to introduce specific genetic traits or modify existing ones. While these technologies hold great promise, they also raise ethical and regulatory considerations that need to be carefully addressed.

Conclusion

Genetics plays a vital role in the practical applications of rabbit breeding. Selective breeding, genetic enhancement, disease resistance, preservation of genetic diversity, and the potential of genetic engineering are all important aspects of genetic improvement in rabbits. By harnessing the power of genetics, breeders can enhance meat production, improve fiber quality, enhance disease resistance, preserve genetic diversity, and explore new possibilities for genetic improvement in the future.

183 The Future of Rabbit Genetics and Breeding Practices

The future of rabbit genetics and breeding practices holds immense promise for advancing our understanding of these remarkable animals and unlocking their full potential for various applications. Here are some key areas where we can expect significant progress:

1. Genetic Diversity and Conservation:

Preserving the genetic diversity of rabbit breeds is crucial for ensuring their resilience and adaptability in the face of environmental changes and disease outbreaks. Advanced genetic tools, such as genome sequencing and marker-assisted selection, will enable researchers and breeders to identify and protect rare and endangered breeds. Collaborative efforts between gene banks, breeding programs, and conservation organizations will be vital in safeguarding the genetic heritage of these animals.

2. Disease Resistance and Health Management:

Rabbit genetics can be harnessed to improve disease resistance and enhance overall health in commercial and pet rabbit populations. By identifying genetic variants associated with susceptibility or resistance to specific diseases, breeders can selectively breed animals with desirable traits. This approach, coupled with advanced diagnostic tools and improved biosecurity measures, will lead to healthier and more robust rabbit populations.

3. Meat and Fur Quality Improvement:

Genetic advancements can significantly improve meat and

fur quality in rabbits. Selective breeding for desirable traits, such as lean muscle mass, growth rate, fur density, and fiber length, will enhance the economic value of these animals for food and fiber production. Additionally, genetic engineering techniques may introduce novel traits, such as disease resistance or improved feed conversion efficiency, further enhancing the industry's sustainability and profitability.

4. Behavioral and Temperament Modification:

Understanding the genetic basis of rabbit behavior and temperament can enable breeders to select animals with desirable traits for different purposes. For example, selecting for calm and docile rabbits can improve their suitability as pets, while breeding for active and exploratory animals may benefit working or show rabbits. Genetic tools can also help identify genetic markers associated with aggression or other undesirable behaviors, allowing for their avoidance in breeding programs.

5. New Rabbit Breeds and Lines:

The future holds exciting possibilities for the development of new rabbit breeds and lines tailored to specific needs. By combining desirable genetic traits from different breeds or introducing novel genetic material through genetic engineering, researchers and breeders can create rabbits with unique characteristics and applications. These new breeds and lines could excel in areas such as meat production, fur quality, disease resistance, or specialized roles in research or conservation.

6. Personalized Breeding and Management:

Advances in genetic testing and data analysis will enable

personalized breeding and management practices for rabbits. By analyzing an individual rabbit's genetic profile, breeders can tailor breeding decisions and management strategies to optimize its potential for specific traits or purposes. This approach will lead to more efficient and targeted breeding programs, resulting in animals that better meet the specific needs of different stakeholders.

7. Ethical and Societal Considerations:

As genetic technologies continue to advance, it is essential to consider the ethical and societal implications of their application in rabbit breeding practices. Open and transparent discussions involving scientists, breeders, animal welfare organizations, and the public will be crucial in establishing guidelines and regulations that ensure the responsible and ethical use of genetic tools for the benefit of rabbits and society as a whole. Advanced genetic technologies, collaborative research efforts, and ethical considerations will shape the direction of this field, leading to significant advancements in preserving genetic diversity, improving health and productivity, modifying behavior, developing new breeds, and personalizing breeding practices. By embracing these advancements, we can unlock the full potential of rabbits for various applications, while ensuring their well-being and respecting ethical boundaries.

Made in the USA
Las Vegas, NV
05 January 2025

15828492R00105